BUSINESS GOALS 3

STUDENT'S BOOK

Gareth Knight   Mark O'Neil   Bernie Hayden

CAMBRIDGE
UNIVERSITY PRESS

CAMBRIDGE UNIVERSITY PRESS
Cambridge, New York, Melbourne, Madrid, Cape Town, Singapore, São Paulo

CAMBRIDGE UNIVERSITY PRESS
The Edinburgh Building, Cambridge CB2 2RU, UK

http://www.cambridge.org
Information on this title: www.cambridge.org/9780521603621

First published 2005

Printed in Italy by Eurografica (part of the LEGO group)

A catalogue record for this book is available from the British Library

ISBN-13 978-0-521-60362-1 Student's Book
ISBN-10 0-521-60362-5 Student's Book

ISBN-13 978-0-521-61785-7 Workbook with Audio CD
ISBN-10 0-521-61785-5 Workbook with Audio CD

ISBN-13 978-0-521-61317-0 Teacher's Book
ISBN-10 0-521-61317-5 Teacher's Book

ISBN-13 978-0-521-61318-7 Audio Cassette
ISBN-10 0-521-61318-2 Audio Cassette

ISBN-13 978-0-521-61319-4 Audio CD
ISBN-10 0-521-61319-1 Audio CD

Contents

Map of the book

On the phone

UNIT GOALS ● contacting companies by phone ● making small talk on the phone

TALKING POINT

Do you feel confident using the telephone …
… in your language?
… in English?
Do you find it easier to make calls or receive them?
Do you think small talk is important on the phone?

PART A Getting through

1 Listening

 Rob Stephens sells health insurance. He is calling three companies – GSK, Logica and Standard – to speak to the Human Resources Director. Listen to the calls and complete the table.

Call	Company name	Successful?	If not successful, why not?
1			
2			
3			

2 Language focus

a) Complete the sentences below from 1 Listening with these phrases.

I'm sorry	Could I have	like to speak	who's calling
it's about	Could I speak	I'll call	It's
put you through	I'm afraid		

1 Hello. I'd .... to the Human Resources Director, please.

2 .... Rob Stephens.

3 Can I ask what .... ?

4 ...., but the director is busy today.

5 .... again.

6 Can I ask ...., please?

7 Thank you. I'll ....

8 .... to Neil Watson, please?

9 .... your name, please?

10 .... Mr Watson isn't available at the moment.

b Listen again and check.

LANGUAGE FILE 1 >> PAGE 84

Communication activity

Student A: Look at the information on page 76.
Student B: Look at the information below.

Situation 1
You work for a company selling office equipment, for example, PCs, fax machines and photocopiers. Look at the business cards.

a Call Hanna Charlton and try to make an appointment.

b Call Jenny Wallis and try to make an appointment.

Hanna Charlton
Purchasing Manager

Perform Pharmaceuticals

National University

Professor Jenny Wallis
Faculty of Computer Science

Situation 2
a You are George H. Swanson's assistant. Look at his business card. Student A will call you to speak to Mr Swanson. Find out who is calling, and why. Put Student A through.

b You are Nadia Clark's assistant. Look at her business card. Student A will call you to speak to Ms Clark. Find out who is calling, and why. Explain that Ms Clark is in a meeting.

 **Corporation**

George H. Swanson
Sales Director

 **SEA Trading Company**

Nadia Clark
General Manager

Exploring

Discuss these questions in pairs.

1 What is 'cold calling'? Choose the best answer:

Calling someone to   a discuss the weather
                   b try and sell something
                   c invite them for a meeting

Is cold calling common in your country?

2 What are the advantages and disadvantages of cold calling (a) for the customer and (b) for the selling company?

3 What do you do when you receive cold calls?

1 Brainstorming

Work in pairs. Make a list of tips for better telephoning.

Example *Give your name at the beginning of the call.*

2 Listening

a   Look at the tips for better telephoning. Compare them with your tips from 1 Brainstorming. Do you agree with them?

> **TELEPHONE TIPS**
>
> a   Always say who you are at the start of the call. ☐
>
> b   Start off with some small talk before you start talking business. ☐
>
> c   Don't let the small talk go on for too long – everybody is busy! ☐
>
> d   Don't end the call too suddenly. ☐

b   Listen to four telephone conversations with communication problems. Which of the four tips above is not followed in each conversation? Write the number of the conversations in the boxes next to the tips.

3 Language focus

a   Listen to another telephone conversation and answer the questions.

1   Who is the caller?

2   What does he want?

3   What does the other person offer to do?

4   Does the conversation follow the four tips above?

b   **Complete the conversation.**

MARCO: Hello. Marco Delta.
CHRIS: Hi, Marco. Chris here.
MARCO: Oh, hi, Chris. How are things?
CHRIS: Not (1) ...., thanks. And (2) ....?
MARCO: Busy, but I (3) .... What (4) .... for you?
CHRIS: Have you got a copy of the latest sales figures?
MARCO: Yes. Shall I email them to you?
CHRIS: That would be great, thanks very much.
MARCO: No problem.
CHRIS: Right, I'll (5) .... Bye for now.
MARCO: Bye, Chris.

c   **Listen again and check.**

LANGUAGE FILE 2 >> PAGE 85

Student A: Look at the information on page 77.
Student B: Look at the information below.

Make two phone calls to Student A using the information below. Prepare what you will say. Remember to make small talk.

Situation 1
You are Lucia Gala. Call Karl Steiner. He has been your customer for three years and you meet several times a year. He has not been well recently. You want to check that he will place a new order shortly.

Situation 2
You are Caroline Jones. Call Beatriz Muñoz. She has been a customer for one year. You have never met, but you talk on the phone regularly. She is studying part-time for her MBA. You are visiting her town next week and would like to make an appointment.

Now look at the information below. Student A will call you. Prepare what you will say.

Situation 3
You are Geoff Graham. You are the Purchasing Manager for your company. You have two young children. Student A is a regular supplier. You get on well with Student A. However, you are very busy with urgent orders. You will place an order with Student A next week when you have more time.

Situation 4
You are Maria Rossi. You are the Sales Director for your company. Student A is a major supplier and you often meet socially. Last week you took Student A out for dinner. You will send a list of samples that you need from Student A by email this week.

⑤ Culture focus

a Look again at the four tips for better telephoning in 2 Listening. Which ones are the same in your company / companies in your country? What other tips would be appropriate in your situation?

b Work in pairs. Tell each other your ideas from (a).

2 Arrangements

UNIT GOALS • writing formal and informal emails • making arrangements

TALKING POINT

What do you use email for? Tick (✓) the boxes.

making arrangements ☐	placing orders ☐
contacting clients ☐	contacting colleagues ☐
chatting to friends ☐	asking for information ☐
giving information ☐	giving invitations ☐

Do you write the same kinds of emails to friends, colleagues and clients? In what ways are they similar and different?

PART A   Writing emails

1 Listening

a Do you think these statements are true (T) or false (F)? Discuss them in pairs.

1 Emails are faster than letters, but more expensive.

2 Email has made business communication less formal.

3 You should use formal language in emails to important customers.

4 You don't need to use a greeting in emails.

5 You should include your contact details at the end of business emails.

◁)) **b Listen to part of a radio interview with John Baxter, an expert in business communication, and check your answers.**

2 Reading

Read the email and answer the questions.

1 Who was the email written to, and what is her job?

2 Who wrote the email, and what is her job?

3 What was her main reason for writing the email?

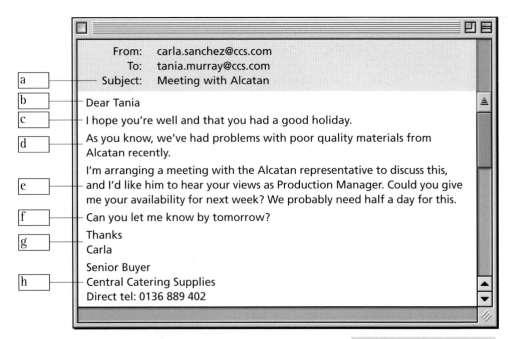

From:	carla.sanchez@ccs.com
To:	tania.murray@ccs.com
a —— **Subject:**	Meeting with Alcatan

b —— Dear Tania

c —— I hope you're well and that you had a good holiday.

d —— As you know, we've had problems with poor quality materials from Alcatan recently.

I'm arranging a meeting with the Alcatan representative to discuss this,
e —— and I'd like him to hear your views as Production Manager. Could you give me your availability for next week? We probably need half a day for this.

f —— Can you let me know by tomorrow?

Thanks
g —— Carla

Senior Buyer
h —— Central Catering Supplies
Direct tel: 0136 889 402

LANGUAGE FILE 1 >> PAGE 86

3 Language focus

a Match the parts of an email 1–8 to the descriptions a–h.

1 Concluding sentence

2 Signing off

3 Subject line

4 Main point

5 Introduction to subject

6 'Signature'

7 Greeting

8 Opening comment

a your position in the company and contact details

b a 'title' that explains what you are writing about

c the most important thing that you want to say

d a friendly personal comment to begin the email

e *Dear* and the other person's name

f this finishes off your message, after your main point

g a brief explanation of what you are writing about

h usually *Best wishes* or *All the best* followed by your name. In less formal emails, this could be *Thanks* followed by your name.

b Label the email in 2 Reading with the headings 1–8 above.

LANGUAGE FILE 2 >> **PAGE 86**

4 Writing

a Read Tania's reply to Carla's email in 2 Reading. In pairs, discuss what is wrong with it.

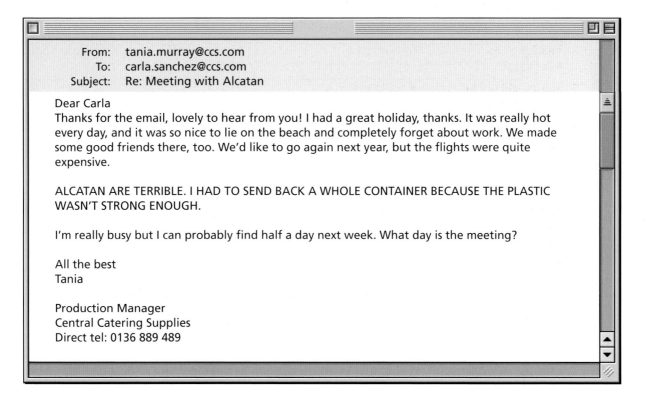

From: tania.murray@ccs.com
To: carla.sanchez@ccs.com
Subject: Re: Meeting with Alcatan

Dear Carla
Thanks for the email, lovely to hear from you! I had a great holiday, thanks. It was really hot every day, and it was so nice to lie on the beach and completely forget about work. We made some good friends there, too. We'd like to go again next year, but the flights were quite expensive.

ALCATAN ARE TERRIBLE. I HAD TO SEND BACK A WHOLE CONTAINER BECAUSE THE PLASTIC WASN'T STRONG ENOUGH.

I'm really busy but I can probably find half a day next week. What day is the meeting?

All the best
Tania

Production Manager
Central Catering Supplies
Direct tel: 0136 889 489

b Rewrite Tania's email to make it a better reply.

1 Reading

a Look at the beginning and ending of two email invitations. Who wrote each email, and who was it written to?

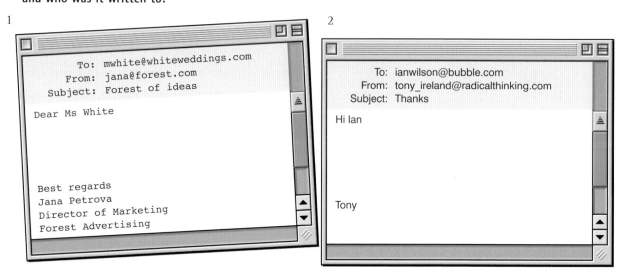

1

> To: mwhite@whiteweddings.com
> From: jana@forest.com
> Subject: Forest of ideas
>
> Dear Ms White
>
>
>
> Best regards
> Jana Petrova
> Director of Marketing
> Forest Advertising

2

> To: ianwilson@bubble.com
> From: tony_ireland@radicalthinking.com
> Subject: Thanks
>
> Hi Ian
>
>
> Tony

b Put these sentences in the correct order to complete email 1.

a ☐ We look forward to seeing you at the fair.

b ☐ I am writing to confirm details of the 'Forest of ideas' fair next month.

c ☐ Please confirm whether you are able to join us for this.

d ☐ The fair will be held at the Marlon Hotel on 17th and 18th May, and we would like to invite you to a special pre-fair dinner for our most valued customers at 8 p.m. on May 16th.

c Put these sentences in the correct order to complete email 2.

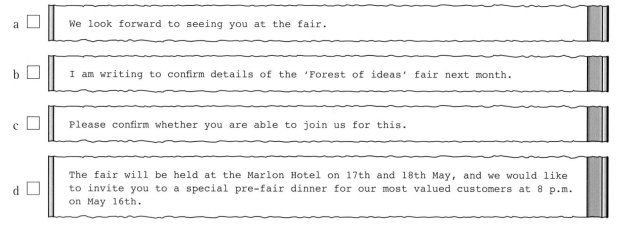

a ☐ Give me a call if you can make it.

b ☐ How about dinner tomorrow night? I can thank you personally and catch up on what's happened to you since your promotion.

c ☐ Thanks for setting up yesterday's meeting for Jane with your boss. I think it was successful. :-)

d ☐ Hope to see you tomorrow.

d Which email is more formal?

2 Language focus

a Match two expressions in email 1 in 1 Reading to similar expressions in email 2.

Example

(Dear) Ms White	(Hi) Ian

b Match the formal expressions 1–7 in the table to the informal expressions a–g.
Complete the table.

a Thanks for the invite.

b Let me know if you can come.

c I'll let you know by Friday.

d Yes, I'd love to come.

e I think I mentioned on the phone, it's on Monday the 29th.

f I'm afraid I can't make it as I've already made plans.

g Do you fancy going out to dinner?

Formal	Informal
Inviting	
1 Would you like to have dinner with us?	
2 As discussed by telephone, the event is on Monday 29th May.	
3 We would be grateful if you could confirm whether you can attend.	
Replying	
4 Thank you for your kind invitation.	
5 I regret I am unable to attend due to a prior engagement.	
6 I can confirm that I will be able to attend.	
7 I will confirm by the end of the week.	

LANGUAGE FILE 3 >> PAGE 88

3 Communication activity

Work in pairs.

Situation 1

a Your publishing company is launching a new business magazine. Write an email to an ex-colleague who you have known for many years. Invite him/her to lunch to discuss the magazine.

b Give your email to another pair. Write a reply to the email you receive.

c Give your reply to the other pair. Read the reply that you receive.

Situation 2

a Write an email to the Director of Marketing at Richmond Finance. You have never met her before. Invite her to the launch of your new business magazine.

b Give your email to another pair. Write a reply to the email you receive.

c Give your reply to the other pair. Read the reply that you receive.

3 Effective communication

UNIT GOALS • making suggestions • expressing opinions • agreeing and disagreeing

How do you usually communicate ...
  ... with friends / other students?
  ... with colleagues in your office / in other offices?
What communication problems can occur in offices?

PART A Ways of communicating

1 Vocabulary

Work in pairs. You are going to listen to two conversations which include these words and phrases. What do you think the conversations will be about?

communicate	isolated	contact
email	impersonal	telephone
video-conferencing		on a regular basis
speed something up		print something out
make copies		

VOCABULARY FILE >> PAGE 90

2 Listening

a Listen to three colleagues discussing problems and check your ideas from 1 Vocabulary.

b Listen again and complete the table.

	Problem	Solution chosen
1		
2		

3 Language focus

a Match the sentence beginnings 1–11 to the endings a–k to make sentences from the conversations in 2 Listening. Then listen again and check.

1	I wonder	a	video-conferencing on the Internet?
2	We want	b	at that then.
3	Have you	c	be a cheap way for us to have face-to-face meetings.
4	I've thought	d	them to feel like part of the team.
5	What about	e	check that they can make copies easily.
6	I think we	f	about it, but it's very expensive.
7	Let's look	g	considered video-conferencing?
8	I think it could	h	like a good solution.
9	Could we	i	could install the software on computers in our offices quite quickly.
10	That sounds	j	email them to the offices as PDF files?
11	We need to	k	if we could communicate a bit better.

b Decide whether each complete sentence is making, accepting or rejecting a suggestion.

LANGUAGE FILE 1 >> PAGE 89

4 Communication activity

Work in pairs. You are both managers at an engineering company. Some employees often work from home, and others are often away on site. You are having a meeting as you are concerned that effective communication is becoming a problem.

STUDENT A: Look at the information on page 77.
STUDENT B: Look at the information below.

Suggest using some of these means of communication, and explain why. Accept or reject Student A's suggestions, and explain why.

Mobile phones:	easy to keep in touch
Laptops:	easy to send/receive emails and attachments from any location
Video-conferencing:	unreliable software on home computers
Two-way radios:	limited distance

1 Reading

a Discuss these questions in pairs.

1 What is a remote worker?

2 What is a virtual team?

3 What are the advantages and disadvantages of virtual teams?

b Read about virtual teams and complete the article with these sentences.

a Don't let remote workers feel they are 'missing out' on something.

b Find ways to compensate for loss of face-to-face contact between colleagues.

c Make senior managers work remotely, at least some of the time.

d Advise employees on how to organize their working environment.

e Visit remote offices frequently and meet as many people as possible.

DOES REMOTE WORKING REALLY WORK?

Some companies see remote working as an easy way to reduce costs and increase productivity. But it's not as simple as that. To create a successful virtual team, it's not enough just to give your employees a laptop and an email account! Business is a highly personal activity, and you cannot replace face-to-face contact with any electronic tool. So, how can you help make it work?

1 .... This helps managers find out what remote working is like, and shows employees that remote working is important for the company right up to senior level.

2 .... Even in a virtual team, it is good to meet employees and customers as often as possible to develop real personal relationships with them.

3 .... Without advice from their company, homeworkers can end up working at the kitchen table and using the same phone line for work and home, and so find it difficult to separate work and home life. Eventually, they become unproductive.

4 .... Encourage phone calls and video-conferencing between colleagues, not just email. Train employees to know when a phone call will be more effective than an email, especially for solving problems and disagreements. Create an online chat room for employees to 'socialize' during breaks.

5 .... Send regular information to remote workers about the company – new employees, job vacancies, etc. – and ask remote workers for their views on company plans.

---

c Do you think virtual teams are a good idea? Are they common in your country?

2 Listening

🔊 **Listen to two managers talking about a virtual team and answer the questions.**

1 What problem does the team have?

2 What four solutions do the managers suggest?

3 Language focus

🔊 **Listen again and complete the expressions used in** 2 Listening.

1 If .... me, our reps in Paris, Madrid, Portugal and Rome should be communicating much more with each other.

2 I .... sharing ideas with each other would make them feel more like part of a team.

3 What ....?

4 I .... more.

5 I .... so, but that would be expensive.

6 Good .... Perhaps we could help them to set up video-conferencing on the Internet.

LANGUAGE FILE 2 >> PAGE 89

4 Communication activity

Work in groups of four. You work for a company based in London, but you all live in different parts of Europe. You are planning to start working as a virtual team, and you are having a meeting in London to discuss the best way to communicate effectively and work efficiently.

STUDENT A: **Look at the information on page 77.**
STUDENT B: **Look at the information on page 78.**
STUDENT C: **Look at the information on page 80.**
STUDENT D: **Look at the information below.**

You live and work in the centre of Warsaw. You like email some of the time. You think personal contact is very important, so you prefer the phone and video-conferencing to email. You would like a meeting every three to six months as it takes a long time to travel to meetings.

Listen to the others' opinions and give yours. Try to agree on a way of working that will be acceptable to all the team.

5 Culture focus

Discuss these questions in pairs.

1 Are virtual teams common in your company / companies in your country?

2 Do you think they work well?

3 Do they fit in with the business culture of your country or company?

Vocabulary 1

Replace the words in italics in the sentences below with these words.

| a prior engagement | Would you like to have | attend | reply | confirm |

1 I would be delighted to *come*.

2 Please *let me know* whether you can come.

3 *How about* dinner next Thursday?

4 I cannot come because of *other plans*.

5 Please *tell me your answer* by the end of the week.

Language 1

Rewrite these telephone phrases to make them more polite.

1 I want to speak to Ms Keppel.

2 Who are you?

3 What do you want?

4 Mr Young is busy.

5 Give me a message.

Communication 1

In pairs, practise conversations using the flow diagram. Student A is the receptionist for MJ Systems. Student B is Pat Clark, a salesperson for EC Limited. Pat Clark calls the manager of MJ Systems. Take turns being the receptionist and Pat Clark.

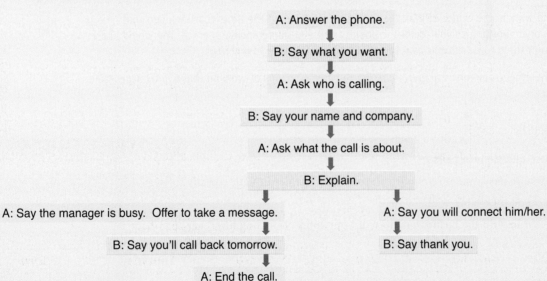

A: Answer the phone.

B: Say what you want.

A: Ask who is calling.

B: Say your name and company.

A: Ask what the call is about.

B: Explain.

A: Say the manager is busy. Offer to take a message.   A: Say you will connect him/her.

B: Say you'll call back tomorrow.   B: Say thank you.

A: End the call.

Vocabulary 2

Complete the puzzle.

Across

3 I'm trying to .... Paul. Have you got his mobile number or email address?

6 That sounds like a good .... Let's try it.

7 Remote workers sometimes feel .... because they work alone.

9 Can you .... out a copy of that report for me?

10 We speak on the .... every day.

11 She didn't get your .... because her PC isn't working.

12 More people work at home now, either on their own or as part of a .... team.

Down

1 We need to .... better with the team, so that they know what's happening.

2 Can you send me a progress report on a .... basis, say once a week?

5, 4 I think ....-.. is better than the phone because you can see the other person.

6 That company's too .... They do everything by email and they never call us.

8 This project's progressing too slowly; we need to .... things up.

Language 2

Put this email in the correct order.

☐
☐
☐
☐
☐

Dear Mr Portman

I would very much like to accept,

I hope it is a very enjoyable evening.

especially as it is the company's centenary,

Thank you very much for your invitation to the annual dinner.

but I am afraid I cannot attend due to a prior engagement.

Regards

Daniel Walters

Communication 2

You want to organize a half-day meeting next week. First, complete this diary page with your availability. Mark three boxes 'free', four boxes 'not free' and three boxes 'possibly free'.

	Monday	Tuesday	Wednesday	Thursday	Friday
a.m.					
p.m.					

Work in groups. Find out everyone's availability and find the best time to have the meeting.

4 Finding work

UNIT GOALS • reading job adverts • writing a covering letter • a job interview

Would you like to work for an international company?

Have you ever had an interview in English for a job?

Would you like to?

PART A Applying for a job

 Reading

a Read the job advertisement and complete these notes.

Job title -

Department -

Location -

Responsibilities -

Skills required -

Experience required -

Qualifications required -

How to apply -

STYLE HOUSE Fashion Accessories

Marketing Executive

We are looking for a dynamic new Marketing Executive to join our busy team. The Marketing Department is based in Manchester in the UK.

Our Marketing Executives are responsible for maintaining the current client base, researching their ongoing requirements and informing the sales and design teams, as well as giving suggestions for promotional activity. You will also be expected to research the market place in order to expand the existing client base, and keep up-to-date with current competition.

Previous experience is not necessary as training will be given. You will be a university graduate (any subject), with a keen interest in the fashion world, good communication and IT skills, a clean driving licence and good time-management skills. You must be self-motivated and able to work to tight deadlines.

This is a permanent position.

To apply, please complete the application form and send it with a covering letter to Martha Chase, Human Resources Director.
Interviews will be held the week of 11th August.

---

b Would you like to apply for this job?
Why / Why not?

2 Language focus

a Read this covering letter written by someone applying for the job opposite.
Look at the advert again. Does the applicant meet all the requirements?

> 38 Steeple Drive
> Marsden
> MD4 8YT
>
> Tel: 08931 462918
>
> Email: kcampbell@mailer.com
>
> Martha Chase
> Human Resources Director
> Style House
> Marsden
> MD2 4BK
>
> 28th July 2005
>
> Dear Ms Chase,
>
> I would like to apply for the post of Marketing Executive advertised in this week's Fashion News.
>
> I have worked as part of the sales team for a fashion designer for six months. I am very interested in the world of fashion and am keen to pursue a career in this area.
>
> I have good communication skills and am able to work both independently and as part of a team. I am self-motivated and can work to tight deadlines. Although I do not have a degree, I have good qualifications from school and excellent computer skills. I have a clean driving licence.
>
> Please find enclosed my CV. If you require any further information, please do not hesitate to contact me.
>
> I look forward to hearing from you.
>
> Yours sincerely,
>
> K Campbell
>
> Kate Campbell
> enc.

b Do you think she is a suitable candidate? Why / Why not?

LANGUAGE FILE 1 >> PAGE 90

3 Writing

Write a covering letter
to apply for this job, which you
saw advertised in last week's
Evening Express.

CUSTOMER SERVICE ADVISOR

Experienced in customer service, you will need excellent communication skills and a friendly, professional approach. You will be able to deal with individuals at all levels and your experience should demonstrate your ability to deal with difficult customer situations.

You will be responsible for ensuring that all orders are placed within the required time, and customers are kept up-to-date on the progress of their orders, and you will arrange delivery of products.

We are a big-name company with a reputation to match, so here's a great opportunity! Call now on 0223 3268439 or write to:

Alan Neill, HR Director
Quicklink
Cambridge CM2 8AD

1 Reading

a Work in pairs. You are going to read an article giving advice about job interviews. What advice do you think it will give under these headings?

Preparation   First impressions   Arrival   During the interview

b Read the article. Compare the advice in the article with the advice you thought of.

HOW TO WIN THE INTERVIEW GAME

Do you get nervous before a job interview? Of course, everybody does. But if you follow our advice, perhaps you won't feel so nervous, and you will probably be more successful!

Preparation
Prepare well. If you know what you want to say in advance, you will be able to express it more clearly in the interview. Identify your skills, interests and career goals before you arrive at the interview. Find out as much as you can about the company – its products or services, number of employees, competitors, problems, etc. This will show your interviewers that you are genuinely interested.

First impressions
It's important to make a good impression, so choose clothes that are appropriate for the company – this may not necessarily be a suit and tie, but you should always wear clothes that convey an image of professionalism and competence. You could take a briefcase or notebook, which will make you look professional, and you could have questions written in your notebook in advance.

Arrival
Don't be late! Being late for your interview could make the interviewer think that punctuality isn't important for you. Aim to arrive 10 to 15 minutes early. Show that you can arrive on time, even if you have had a long journey.

During the interview
Be polite and friendly with the interviewer, even if he/she annoys you – it could be a test of how you react to pressure! Establish a rapport with the interviewer by using eye contact, facial expressions and gestures to show that you understand what he/she is saying. Try to look enthusiastic and confident – for example, avoid moving around too much in your chair, which will make you look nervous and uncomfortable.
Pause slightly before answering a question, to give yourself time to prepare your answer. Answer questions directly and fully. Don't just say 'Yes' or 'No', but don't go on for too long either! Listen to questions carefully; speak clearly and confidently. Be positive about yourself and your background – if the interviewer asks what you think your negative points are (a common question), say just one or two things, then say what you are doing or have done to improve in these areas. And don't say anything negative about your past jobs or employers!

c Read the article again and say if these statements are true (T) or false (F) according to the article.

1 Some people don't feel nervous before a job interview.

2 Before the interview, you should decide what to say about yourself.

3 You should always wear a suit and tie for an interview.

4 If you have travelled a long way, it is all right to arrive late.

5 You should try to sit fairly still in your chair.

6 Say positive things about yourself and your past employers.

2 Listening

🔊 **a** Listen to Sara being interviewed for a job.

Tick (✓) the positive points she mentions about herself.

creative ☐ self-motivated ☐ highly skilled ☐ realistic ☐

dynamic ☐ flexible ☐ ambitious ☐ hard-working ☐

expert ☐ dedicated ☐

b Do you think Sara is a good candidate? Why / Why not?

3 Language focus

a Match the questions and answers from the interview in 1 Listening.

1 What have you got to offer us?

2 What do you think your negative points are?

3 What is it about this post that attracts you?

4 Where do you see yourself five years from now?

5 Have you ever used the Quaddro system?

6 Do you have any questions for me?

a Yes, I have. I haven't used it in my current job, as the company uses Mekra.

b I would like to be the manager of a whole division in five years.

c Yes, I have one or two written down here.

d I'm creative and dynamic – I think my track record in my current job proves that.

e I think this post offers a good opportunity to develop my skills.

f Perhaps I don't always delegate as much as I should.

🔊 **b** Listen again and check.

LANGUAGE FILE 2 >> **PAGE 92**

4 Communication activity

a Work in pairs. Role play the following situation.

STUDENT A: You have applied for the Sales Manager job advertised here and Student B is going to interview you. Prepare for your interview. Make notes about your skills, qualifications and experience. Think about how you could answer the questions in Language file 2 on page 92.

STUDENT B: You are a Human Resources Manager. You are going to interview Student A for the Sales Manager job advertised here. Prepare questions to ask. Use Language file 2 on page 92 to help you.

b Change roles and practise again, using the IT Support Team Manager job advertised here.

SALES MANAGER – OFFICE EQUIPMENT

We are looking for a dynamic person to manage our sales team.

You must have a smart appearance, be ambitious, self-motivated and have good communication skills.

You must be literate and numerate, have good IT skills and a good level of education.

Experience is preferred, but not essential as full training will be given.

IT SUPPORT TEAM MANAGER –
ACCOUNTANCY FIRM

We are looking for a manager for our busy IT support team.

You must be dynamic and hard-working with good communication skills and, of course, excellent IT skills!

Previous experience in IT support essential. University degree preferred.

5 Working with others

UNIT GOALS • asking for permission • giving and refusing permission • delegating

How easy is it to ask for permission …
  … to go home early?
  … to take a day off?
Who do you usually ask permission from at work/college?

PART A   Getting permission

1 Vocabulary

a Match these words and phrases to the verbs below.

> a day off   home early   time off   late
> to the dentist   at home   a holiday
> the time up   a personal call

take   *a day off*
....
....

work   ....

go   *home early*
....

make   ....
....

b Which of the things above do you need to ask permission for at work/college?

VOCABULARY FILE >> **PAGE 95**

2 Listening

a Listen to five short conversations between employees and their managers. Underline the requests that you hear.

1 finish early ☐   5 have an extended deadline ☐
2 have a day off ☐   6 work at home ☐
3 go to the dentist ☐   7 go to the doctor ☐
4 work overtime ☐   8 make a personal call ☐

b Listen again. Tick (✓) the requests the employees get permission for. Put a cross (✗) next to the requests they don't get permission for. Why don't they get permission?

3 Language focus

a Work in pairs. Put the two conversations in the correct order.

1

- [ ] At 9.15. I can work later in the evening, if that's OK.
- [ ] Oh, dear. What is it?
- [ ] I need to take my daughter to school in the mornings for a couple of weeks, and I was wondering if I could come in a bit later than usual.
- [ ] I'll see what I can do.
- [1] Jane, I've got a bit of a problem.
- [ ] I'm sorry, Ken. The problem is that the regular meetings often start at 9.00. Is there any other way round it?
- [ ] That could be a problem. What time will you come in?

2

- [ ] Sure. What is it?
- [ ] About 4.45.
- [ ] Fine. No problem.
- [ ] I suppose so. Anything wrong?
- [1] Paul, do you have a minute?
- [ ] No, nothing's wrong. I have a dentist's appointment, that's all.
- [ ] OK. What time do you need to leave?
- [ ] Thanks a lot.
- [ ] Could I leave a bit early today?

b Listen to the conversations and check.

c Work in pairs. Have conversations using the requests in 2 Listening**. Take turns to be the manager and the employee.**

LANGUAGE FILE 1 >> **PAGE 94**

4 Communication activity

STUDENT A: **Look at the information on page 76.**
STUDENT B: **Look at the information below.**

Situation 1
You are an employee. Student A is your manager. You need specialized dental treatment. You need to go to the dentist every Tuesday morning for the next five weeks. Each appointment will take two and a half hours. The dentist is a specialist and is only available on Tuesday mornings. Ask for permission.

Situation 2
You are a manager. Student A is your employee and wants to ask you something. Listen to the request and ask questions to get more details if necessary. Refuse the request for every Friday, as staff need to be in the office then. Suggest that you will decide on a weekly basis, depending on how busy the office is.

5 Writing

Your car has broken down and will be in the garage for at least a week. Because there are very few buses from your town to the office, you will have to arrive for work late and finish early every day. Your manager is in meetings all day so you cannot speak to him. Write an email to your manager asking for permission.

1 Reading

a **Read the article about delegating and match the questions 1–5 to the paragraphs a–e.**

1 Are there any disadvantages?

2 How should you delegate?

3 Why delegate?

4 Who should you delegate to?

5 What is delegating?

The art of delegating

a   Delegating means giving some of your tasks and responsibilities to the people who work for you.

b   Delegating gives employees more responsibility, which motivates them to work harder. It also helps employees learn faster and develop more quickly into possible managers. Delegating helps managers because they don't have to do everything themselves, and they have more time to concentrate on 'the big picture' and check how things are going.

c   It can take longer to tell others what to do than to do something yourself. And managers sometimes worry that the job won't get done, or at least not the way that they would like. But the more managers delegate, the more efficient everyone becomes!

d   Choose tasks for people according to their abilities and how much time they have. You could let people choose – if they are interested in a particular task, they should be motivated to do it well. Don't always give the most important tasks to the most successful employees; this is like punishing them with more work.

e   Separate work logically, so that each person has reasonable and complete tasks. Clearly explain what needs to be done, and why. Explain how to do the task. Give deadlines, and set up systems where employees can check their own progress, so that you don't have to check work in too much detail. Give constructive feedback – praise in public, criticize in private.

b **Read the article again. Are these statements true (T) or false (F)?**

1 Delegating includes giving some of your tasks to other people.

2 Delegating makes work more difficult for employees.

3 Delegating allows managers to check progress more easily.

4 Managers should give longer instructions to employees.

5 Managers should not let employees decide which tasks to do.

6 The best employees should always do the most important tasks.

7 Managers should set deadlines for tasks.

8 Managers should give all feedback in public.

c **Do you agree with everything the article says?**

2 Listening

a Which tasks in the table do you think a manager should do, and which should he/she delegate?

	Task	Delegate? Yes/No?	Reason
1	Meet a new client for the first time.		
2	Write a monthly departmental progress report.		
3	Write a progress report on a specific area in the department.		
4	Take the minutes of a departmental meeting.		

b Listen to four managers talking about the tasks and complete the table. Do they delegate the tasks? Why / Why not?

3 Language focus

a Listen to two conversations in which managers delegate tasks. In each conversation, what is the task, and when can the person do it?

b Who said what? Fill in the table with the numbers of these sentences. Then listen again and check.

1 Howard, could you do something for me this morning?

2 OK. I'll let you know when I've heard from everyone.

3 I'm a bit busy right now, but I could do it in about an hour. What is it?

4 Can you get back to me when you've set it up?

5 Sure. What day do you want to have the meeting?

6 Jenny, I was wondering if you could do some research for me.

7 Er, yes, I think I could ... but how soon do you need it?

8 Would you contact all the Sales Managers ...?

Manager (request)	Employee (response)

LANGUAGE FILE 2 >> **PAGE 95**

4 Communication activity

Work in pairs.

STUDENT A: **You are a manager. Ask Student B to do one of the urgent tasks below.**

STUDENT B: **You are a staff member. You cannot do the task immediately. Discuss how and when the task can be completed.**

• Prepare a report on this month's sales figures.

• Write an email to all employees announcing a new member of staff.

• Make a list of all office computer equipment, to send to Head Office.

• Prepare a factory tour for a new supplier who's visiting.

Choose another task from the list and change roles.

6 Performance at work

UNIT GOALS • giving and receiving feedback • responding to feedback

TALKING POINT

Does your manager or teacher give you feedback on your work? How?

What are the advantages of getting feedback?

Do you think it's difficult giving feedback? Why / Why not?

PART A   Feedback

1 Vocabulary

Match the verbs 1–7 to the words a–g.

1 meet/miss/set a	5 deal with	a with solutions	e a target
2 set	6 come up	b the budget	f the team
3 go	7 stay within	c over budget	g problems
4 support		d deadline	

VOCABULARY FILE >> **PAGE 97**

2 Listening

Paula is the Product Manager of an office equipment manufacturer. She works at Head Office in the UK. The company has recently launched a new product in Italy, and Marco was the Project Manager. Listen to Paula giving feedback to Marco and answer the questions.

1 What did Marco do well?

2 What problems were there?

3 What suggestions does Paula make?

4 Was the project successful?

3 Language focus

a Match Paula's comments 1–6 to Marco's responses a–f.

1 We were pleased that you set realistic targets.

2 It was also good that you dealt with problems quickly.

3 Spending control could have been better.

4 You could have more frequent budget reviews.

5 Some team members didn't always know what was happening. You need to improve team communication.

6 Have you thought of sending out weekly email updates to the whole team?

a Well, as you know, I like the problem-solving side of things.

b Yes, the budgets are so tight these days ... Have you got any suggestions for dealing with that?

c No, but that sounds good. I'll try that next time.

d I was, too. That can be quite hard sometimes.

e Mmm, well, it was a big project team. What could I do about that?

f Yes, that's a good idea. Thanks for that.

b Listen again and check.

c Match these headings to sentences 1–6 above.

Praise ☐ ☐   Negative feedback ☐ ☐   Suggestions ☐ ☐

LANGUAGE FILE 1 >> **PAGE 96**

4 Communication activity

STUDENT A: **Look at the information on page 78.**
STUDENT B: **Look at the information below.**

Situation 1

You are a Project Manager for a large design and manufacturing company. Student A is one of your Team Leaders in another country. You both worked on a project that has recently been completed, and you have arranged to call Student A to give feedback.

a **Look at your notes. Think about what to say, and think of some suggestions for those areas that need to be improved.**

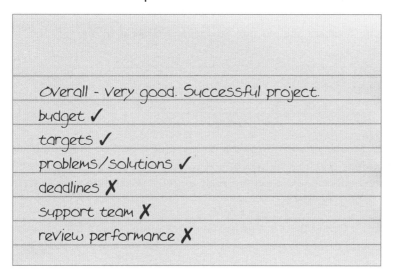

```
Overall - very good. Successful project.
budget ✓
targets ✓
problems/solutions ✓
deadlines ✗
support team ✗
review performance ✗
```

b **Call Student A and give your feedback.**

Situation 2

You are a freelance Project Manager. Student A is a Product Manager in another country. You both worked on a project that has recently been completed, and Student A has arranged to call you to give feedback. You met all your deadlines, but the project went over budget.

a **Think about what Student A might say about these things, and how you could ask for suggestions.**

- budgets
- deadlines
- problems and solutions
- reviewing performance
- supporting the team
- targets

b **Answer Student A's call and discuss your feedback.**

5 Culture focus

Discuss these questions in groups.

1 Is it common for managers to give feedback in your company / companies in your country?

2 Do managers talk about positive things first, then the negative?

3 Are managers very direct in their criticisms?

4 Do managers offer constructive suggestions?

1 Reading

a   **Work in pairs. Look at these statements about dealing with feedback. Discuss what they mean and decide whether you agree with them.**

1   Explain what you want.

2   Be understanding with the person giving feedback.

3   Keep cool.

4   The more feedback the better.

b   **Read the article giving advice about feedback and put the statements 1–4 above in the right part of the text.**

Handling feedback at work

a   .... You should always ask for lots of feedback so that you become better at handling it, and you may also find out something useful. Some people are not keen to criticize so if you ask for more feedback, you are more likely to get it. Make sure you ask frequently, so that people get used to offering feedback.

b   .... Remember that giving feedback is often more difficult than receiving it, and most people find it hard to give honest feedback. Encourage your evaluators and thank them.

c   .... Make your request for feedback more specific. Ask: 'What can I do to improve?' rather than: 'How am I doing?' Or: 'What would you like me to do more/less often?' rather than: 'Was my performance good?' Give people time to prepare their feedback: 'I'd like some feedback. Could we talk next week?'

d   .... It is hard to remain calm when someone is criticizing you. Remember that honest feedback is for your own benefit and may save you a lot of pain later on. Feedback (whether it is good or bad) is a tool that will help you develop.

2 Listening

a   **Listen to three managers giving feedback. Match the criticisms below to the conversations 1–3.**

Some of the work was completed late.   ☐

Some of the team didn't get enough help.   ☐

The team weren't in contact with each other enough.   ☐

b   **Listen again. How did the staff member respond to the criticism in each case? Match the types of response to the conversations 1–3.**

He/She rejected the criticism.   ☐

He/She asked for more details.   ☐

He/She accepted the criticism.   ☐

3 Language focus

Match the headings 1–6 to the expressions a–f from 2 Listening.

1 Accepting criticism
2 Apologizing
3 Offering a solution
4 Asking for more details
5 Rejecting criticism
6 Giving reasons

a I'm not sure that's entirely fair.
b Yes, that's true.
c I did my best but we didn't always receive the information ...
d In future, I'll plan extra training ...
e I'm sorry about that.
f I'm not exactly sure what you mean. Can you give me specific examples?

LANGUAGE FILE 2 >> PAGE 97

4 Communication activity

a Read this email from a manager giving feedback. What are the good points and what are the criticisms?

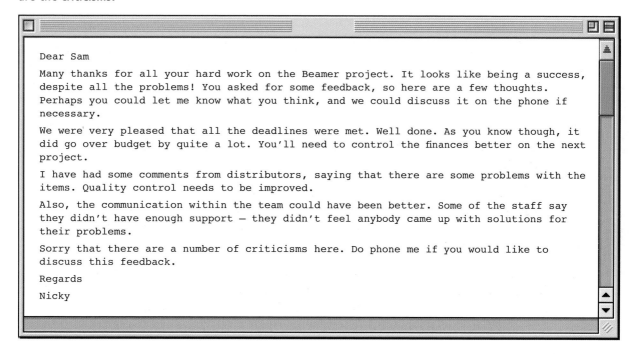

Dear Sam

Many thanks for all your hard work on the Beamer project. It looks like being a success, despite all the problems! You asked for some feedback, so here are a few thoughts. Perhaps you could let me know what you think, and we could discuss it on the phone if necessary.

We were very pleased that all the deadlines were met. Well done. As you know though, it did go over budget by quite a lot. You'll need to control the finances better on the next project.

I have had some comments from distributors, saying that there are some problems with the items. Quality control needs to be improved.

Also, the communication within the team could have been better. Some of the staff say they didn't have enough support – they didn't feel anybody came up with solutions for their problems.

Sorry that there are a number of criticisms here. Do phone me if you would like to discuss this feedback.

Regards

Nicky

b Work in pairs.

STUDENT A: **You are Sam. You decide to phone Nicky to discuss her feedback. Prepare what to say about each point – accept the criticism, reject it, give a reason or ask for more details.**

STUDENT B: **You are Nicky. Prepare to respond to what Sam might say about your feedback.**

c Role play the phone conversation between Sam and Nicky. Then change roles and practise again.

5 Writing

Write an email replying to Nicky. Include the following:
- thank Nicky for the feedback
- accept one criticism and offer a solution
- ask for more details about one criticism

Vocabulary 1

Decide if each item below is something that the employee needs permission for (P), or something that the boss could delegate (D) or both (B).

1 take a day off ☐
2 submit a report late ☐
3 research new suppliers ☐
4 send a memo ☐
5 work at home ☐
6 request a report ☐

7 plan a sales campaign ☐
8 buy a new PC ☐
9 make personal calls ☐
10 take a long lunch ☐
11 send out new catalogues ☐
12 arrange a meeting ☐

Language 1

Match the requests 1–6 to the responses a–f.

1 Could I have a day off tomorrow, please?
2 Can you finish the report by tomorrow evening?
3 I'd like you to do some photocopying for me.
4 Can you wait until Friday for the report?
5 Mr Sante is coming today. Can you meet him?
6 My PC has a virus. Can someone check it for me?

a I'm sorry, I'm out today.
b Yes. Call IT right away.
c I should be able to do it today, in fact.
d Certainly. When do you need it done?
e Friday at the latest, please.
f Is it important?

Communication 1

Work in pairs. You both work in the same office, and below is a list of tasks to be done today. Student A is the manager, and Student B is one of the employees.

STUDENT A: Decide which tasks you will do, and which ones you would like Student B to do. Then try and delegate these tasks to Student B. Note who is going to do each task.

STUDENT B: Decide which tasks you can do, and which tasks you would prefer not to do, and why. Then listen to Student A's requests, and say whether you can do each one or not. Note who is going to do each task.

Attend the weekly meeting with the director.

Have meetings with clients.

Send brochures to clients.

Answer the telephone.

Write replies to email requests.

Plan the sales campaign.

Place advertisements in newspapers.

Role play the situation. Then change roles and practise again with a different partner.

Vocabulary 2

a Find nine words in the puzzle that could be used when giving feedback.

b Complete these phrases with words from the puzzle.

1 keep people *motivated*

2 meet a _ _ _ _ _ _ _ _

3 achieve a _ _ _ _ _ _

4 go over _ _ _ _ _ _

5 support the _ _ _ _

6 deal with _ _ _ _ _ _ _ _

7 come up with _ _ _ _ _ _ _ _ _

8 review _ _ _ _ _ _ _ _

9 recommend _ _ _ _ _ _ _ _ _ _ _

F	M	I	S	M	O	T	I	V	A	T	E	D
B	A	J	O	E	N	E	M	W	S	A	V	E
D	D	O	L	T	T	X	P	R	D	R	T	A
X	E	B	P	A	S	M	R	I	F	G	K	J
A	A	Z	R	B	P	R	O	G	R	E	S	S
U	D	C	O	Q	E	C	V	L	G	T	E	D
F	L	O	B	U	D	G	E	T	D	E	R	G
N	I	L	L	A	R	H	M	A	N	A	G	O
B	N	L	E	X	E	R	E	K	N	I	T	T
T	E	A	M	L	C	X	N	E	T	V	E	I
W	P	Y	S	O	L	U	T	I	O	N	S	D
S	I	M	O	R	A	W	S	T	D	P	K	W

Language 2

Look at the headings a–d and responses to criticism 1–6. Put a, b, c or d in the boxes.

a Accepting criticism

b Giving reasons

c Rejecting criticism

d Asking for more details

1 I understand, but I don't think it was my responsibility. ☐

2 Can you be more specific about the complaint? ☐

3 I'll have to work on this area and make improvements. ☐

4 I see your point, but I think there are other factors. ☐

5 That's a valid point. Let me think about what I can do. ☐

6 I think you may be expecting too much from me. ☐

Communication 2

Work in pairs. Think of a job that you are both interested in or know something about. Prepare for an interview for that job.

STUDENT A: You are the interviewer. Prepare questions for Student B about, for example: experience; time in current job; why leaving; why this job; good points; negative points; plans three years from now.

STUDENT B: You are the interviewee. Prepare answers about yourself, or someone you know, or make them up. Think about: experience; time in current job; why leaving; why this job; good points; negative points; plans three years from now. Think of some questions to ask.

Role play the interview. Then change roles and practise again with a different partner.

7 | Business media

UNIT GOALS • reading and summarizing business news • talking about business news
• getting information from the Internet

How do you find out about business news – from TV, radio, newspapers, the Internet? Which do you prefer, and why? Do you use the Internet for your work or studies? What do you like and dislike about it?

PART A   Talking about the news

1 Reading

a Read the news stories below and match them to these headlines.

1 | National airline reports big increase in profits

2 | Internet search engine doubles market share

3 | Low-cost airline passenger numbers rising

4 | Internet search engine pair join 'richest' list

5 | Good figures for aircraft builder

a The UK-based budget airline easyJet has announced that passenger numbers have gone up by nearly a fifth. The airline carried 1.86 million people in February, a rise of 17.4% compared to the same month last year. Chief Executive Ray Webster said that these figures confirm his comments at the recent AGM, when he said, 'We remain cautiously optimistic regarding our performance for the full financial year.'

b The creators of Internet search engine Google have joined the *Forbes* magazine list of world billionaires. With $1 billion each, Sergey Brin and Larry Page are among many new additions to the list, which has 587 names this year compared with 476 last year. Microsoft chairman Bill Gates topped the list for the tenth consecutive year with an estimated wealth of $46.6 billion.

c European plane maker EADS made a profit last year, after heavy losses the year before. It achieved net profits of €152,000,000, helped by a big increase in deliveries during the second half of the year. The firm, home of the Airbus passenger jets, overtook its US rival Boeing for the first time in the thirty-year history of the Airbus.

d Ask Jeeves, the Internet search engine, has agreed to buy Interactive Search Holdings for $328 million. This will increase its market share from 3.5% to 7%, and make it a more significant competitor to Google and Yahoo. Google has already seen its share of the market go down from 80% to 50%, as Yahoo stops using Google technology.

e Pre-tax profits at British Airways (BA) have risen to £230m for this year, from £135m last year. But BA warned that rising oil costs, which have already pushed up ticket prices, would raise costs by £150m this year. Chief Executive Rod Eddington said, 'When fuel prices go up like this, you can't really hide from them.'

b Choose the correct alternatives and read the stories again to check. Then compare with a partner.

1 In February, easyJet carried nearly:

   a one million passengers   b two million passengers   c three million passengers

2 easyJet's passenger numbers went up by nearly:

   a 20%   b 5%   c 40%.

3 Sergey Brin has:

   a a million dollars   b half a billion dollars   c a billion dollars

4 Bill Gates has:

   a nearly 45 billion dollars   b over 45 billion dollars   c exactly 45 billion dollars

5 Compared to the year before, EADS' performance last year was:

   a better   b worse   c the same

6 Compared to Boeing, EADS' performance last year was:

   a better   b worse   c the same

7 Ask Jeeves' market share is going to:

   a go down   b go up   c stay the same

8 Google's market share has:

   a gone down   b gone up   c stayed the same

9 This year, BA made:

   a more money   b less money   c the same amount of money

10 BA's fares have:

   a stayed the same   b gone down   c gone up

2 Language focus

a Listen to two conversations about the news stories in 1 Reading. **Which stories are they talking about – a, b, c, d or e?**

b Listen again and complete the conversations.

1

A: .... those two guys who started ....?

B: No, ... them?

A: They've both .... now.

B: ....? Where .... that?

A: In the paper. They're in *Forbes* magazine's list of billionaires.

B: Imagine having all that money!

2

A: Hey, this ....

B: What ....?

A: .... passenger numbers ....

B: That ...., actually.

A: Why?

B: Well, ... were hoping to make a good profit this year.

LANGUAGE FILE 1 >> PAGE 98

3 Communication activity

STUDENT A: **Look at the information on page 79.**
STUDENT B: **Look at the information on page 80.**

1 Vocabulary

Match the words 1–7 to the definitions a–g.

1	search	a	move up and down the page
2	browse	b	a place where you click to go to another web page
3	home page	c	look for something specific by typing it in a box
4	menu	d	look around a website to see what it contains
5	drop-down menu	e	a list of things to choose from
6	link	f	the opening page of a website
7	scroll	g	a list which appears when you click on an arrow

VOCABULARY FILE >> PAGE 99

2 Reading

a Read the three web pages a–c and match them to these topics.

1 Accommodation

2 News

3 Travel

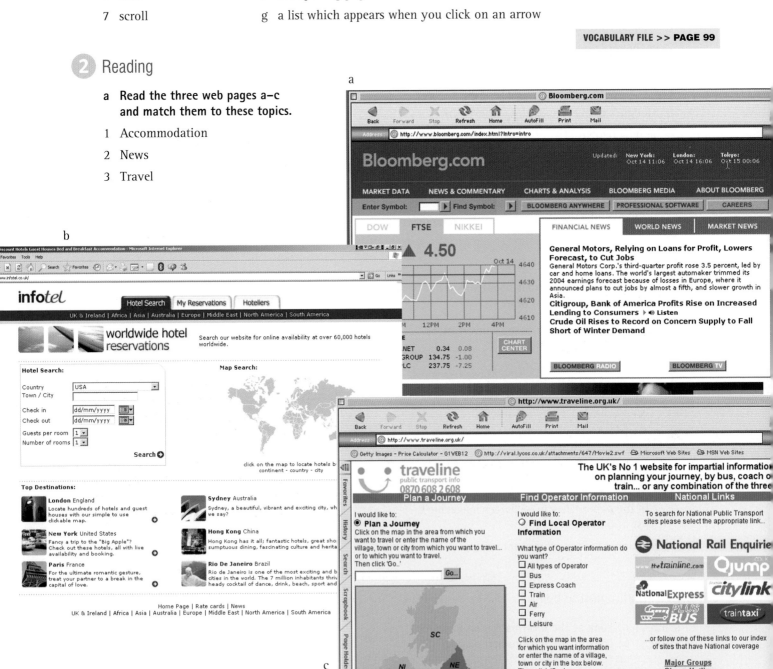

b Read the web pages again and answer the questions.

Which web page(s) has(have) ...

1 ... a clickable map?

2 ... links to other companies?

3 ... links to other media?

4 ... links to information about different countries?

5 ... a link for contacting the company?

3 Listening

Listen to a conversation about one of the websites in 2 Reading and answer these questions.

1 What does the man want to do?

2 Which website is recommended?

3 What questions does the man ask about the website?

4 Language focus

Listen again to the conversation in 3 Listening and complete what the woman says.

1 Well, you .... bus, coach and train times, and choose the best way.

2 There's a .... your town or, if you prefer, there's a .... of the UK.

3 There are .... the train and coach companies for their specific journey planners.

LANGUAGE FILE 2 >> **PAGE 98**

5 Culture focus

a Read the text and answer the questions.

1 What kinds of websites are American office workers looking at during work time?

2 What are the advantages and disadvantages of surfing websites at work?

Keeping up-to-date or just wasting time?

In a recent survey, more than 30% of American office workers said that they spend time at work surfing websites that are nothing to do with work. But is this a bad thing?

Some say that it is important to keep up with the news, culture and changes in technology. "Keeping up-to-date helps me to do my job well," said one employee.

Others believe that workers shouldn't be allowed to browse the Internet. "People shouldn't be wasting valuable time by following their personal interests," said one employer.

b Discuss these questions in pairs.

1 Do you think surfing the Internet is wasting company time? Why / Why not?

2 Does this happen in your company / companies in your country?

8 Meetings

UNIT GOALS • following meetings • taking notes at meetings • taking part in a meeting

TALKING POINT

Do you think meetings are useful?
  Why / Why not?
What do you need to know about a meeting before it starts?
How useful is it to make notes during a meeting?

PART A **The agenda and minutes**

 Vocabulary

Match some of the words from the agenda to the descriptions below.

Funcam

Product development meeting
Wednesday 23rd August 10.00 – 12.00
Room B 317
Chair: Tony Stanton

AGENDA

1. Apologies
2. Minutes
3. Matters arising
4. Sales report
5. Product updates
6. Relaunch of Max Fun model
7. AOB
8. Next meeting

a discussion of points from the last meeting

b notes showing what was discussed at the last meeting

c this is where you arrange when the group will meet again

d explanations from people who cannot attend

e discussion of points not named in the agenda ('any other business')

f a full list of what will be discussed

g the person who manages the meeting

VOCABULARY FILE >> PAGE 101

2 Reading

a What is the purpose of minutes?

b Read two different versions of the minutes for item 5 from the agenda in 1 Vocabulary. Which one is better, 1 or 2? Why?

1

We all talked about current products a lot, and looked at the results of the Funcam single use camera and the Executive camera, which are both declining, and the Mini-digital camera, which is growing steadily. We looked at the sales figures and then looked at the forecasts for the following year, which are more positive than the figures for this year. So, the marketing person will continue doing market research on how to improve sales and the salesperson will send monthly sales figures to staff.

2

5. Product updates

Funcam single use camera, Executive camera and Mini-digital camera
• Sales figures
• Forecasts for following year
Action:
David Miles (Marketing) – Continue to do market research on these products by 20th September.
Sonia Collins (Sales) – Keep staff posted with monthly sales figures.

LANGUAGE FILE 1 >> **PAGE 100**

3 Listening

a Listen to a discussion about item 6 on the agenda in 1 Vocabulary and choose the correct alternatives.

1 Sales of the Max Fun are:
  a going down
  b going up
  c staying the same

2 Tony suggests that Ana does:
  a direct marketing
  b Internet searches
  c market research

3 Ana's task will take:
  a less than a month
  b more than a month
  c more than six weeks

4 John suggests:
  a changing the cost of the camera
  b finding out how much it will cost to make changes
  c finding out why the cost of the camera has changed

5 Clare is going to investigate:
  a three new colour waterproof versions
  b two new colours and a waterproof version
  c three new colours and a waterproof version

6 John's team will provide new packaging ideas in:
  a three or four weeks
  b thirty-four weeks
  c three or four days

b Listen again and write down the key points from the meeting: names, problems, action points and dates.

4 Writing

Work in pairs. Use your notes from 3 Listening to write minutes for item 6 on the agenda in 1 Vocabulary.

1 Brainstorming

Work in pairs. Make a list of reasons why meetings are not always successful.

2 Reading

a Read these comments about meetings. Compare them with your ideas in 1 Brainstorming.

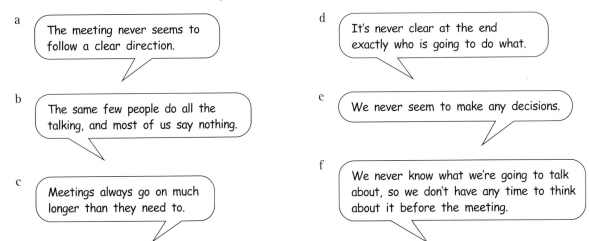

a
The meeting never seems to follow a clear direction.

b
The same few people do all the talking, and most of us say nothing.

c
Meetings always go on much longer than they need to.

d
It's never clear at the end exactly who is going to do what.

e
We never seem to make any decisions.

f
We never know what we're going to talk about, so we don't have any time to think about it before the meeting.

b Read this article about meetings and match the pieces of advice 1–6 to the comments a–f above.

Everyone complains about having too many meetings! But in fact, if the meetings are useful, people don't mind. Here are a few tips for successful meetings:

1 Always send an agenda to all participants well in advance.

2 Set a time limit for the meeting, and keep to it. If you haven't finished discussing everything, stop. That way you will learn to keep within your time limits in future.

3 Keep to the agenda. Don't 'wander off' into other topics of discussion not on the agenda.

4 For each point on the agenda, invite each person to speak in turn. If someone has nothing to contribute on a particular point, he or she can say that.

5 For each point on the agenda, make sure that a decision is reached, and that everyone knows what that decision is. Include all decisions in the minutes.

6 For each point on the agenda, state clearly if there is an action point, and check that everyone knows who is going to carry out the action, and when. Include all action points in the minutes.

3 Listening

Listen to part of a meeting in which senior managers discuss ways of cutting costs and decide whether these statements are true (T) or false (F).

1 Anne-Marie says that cutting employee numbers is the best way to reduce costs.

2 Ben thinks the company has too many skilled workers at the moment.

3 Ben says the company makes too many different products.

4 Anne-Marie thinks they can reduce production without cutting employees.

5 Ben says that if they focus on the bestselling products, they could increase staff.

6 Chris summarizes the key points of the discussion.

7 Chris suggests that Ben does his research after Anne-Marie has finished hers.

8 Anne-Marie and Ben both agree with Chris's suggestions.

4 Language focus

Match the halves to make complete sentences from 3 Listening.

1 I'm not sure   a quite with you.

2 Sorry, Ben, I'm not   b focusing on the bestsellers, we can reduce costs.

3 Can we just go   c over what you're both saying?

4 You're saying that by   d more savings by simply reducing the workforce.

5 You think we would make   e I understand what you mean.

LANGUAGE FILE 2 >> PAGE 100

5 Communication activity

Work in groups of four. You all work for a soft drinks company. Sales of your leading brand have been falling steadily for some time, and you are having a meeting to discuss:

- why this has happened
- what the company needs to do about it
- who should do what

STUDENT A: Look at the information on page 78.
STUDENT B: Look at the information on page 80.
STUDENT C: Look at the information on page 82.
STUDENT D: Look at the information below.

You are the Design Director. You think sales have gone down because people have got bored with the packaging and the style of presentation. You think the product should be relaunched with a new design, new packaging and a new image.

Introduce yourself, give your opinions, listen to the others' opinions and then try to agree on the best course of action.

6 Culture focus

The advice in 2 Reading is for a successful meeting in the UK or the US. Does the same advice apply to meetings in your company / companies in your country?

UNIT

9 | Time management

UNIT GOALS • discussing schedules • planning a trip • changing arrangements

TALKING POINT

How do you plan your time for your work or studies? Do you think you manage your time well? Why / Why not? What plans do you make before going on a trip? What problems could you have?

PART A | Planning schedules

 **Vocabulary**

a Match the verbs 1–6 to the words a–f. Some words go with more than one verb.

1 make	a a deadline
2 keep	b a list
3 meet/miss/set	c on time
4 run	d behind schedule
5 put in	e up-to-date
6 keep something	f extra time

b Do this quiz. Then work in pairs and ask each other the questions.

HOW'S YOUR
TIME MANAGEMENT?
DO OUR QUIZ AND FIND OUT!

How often do you ...

1	... keep up-to-date with your work?	a always	b sometimes	c never
2	... make a daily list of your tasks?	a always	b sometimes	c never
3	... make a list of tasks in order of importance?	a always	b sometimes	c never
4	... do small, unimportant tasks before bigger, more important ones?	a never	b sometimes	c always
5	... keep a record of how long it takes you to complete your tasks?	a always	b sometimes	c never
6	... leave big tasks to the last minute?	a never	b sometimes	c always
7	... miss a deadline?	a never	b sometimes	c always
8	... put in extra time at work?	a always	b sometimes	c never

Add up your score: a = 2 points, b = 1 point, c = 0 points. Your total: ☐

Now turn to page 45 to see what your score means.

VOCABULARY FILE 1 >> PAGE 102

2 Listening

a Listen to Harry, a sales representative, describing his plans for the next three months to Ursula, his manager. Are these statements true (T) or false (F)?

1 The goal is to find new customers.

2 Harry wants a list of companies who didn't buy anything last year.

3 He'd like to visit every company on his list in two months.

4 He thinks he should visit some companies twice.

b Listen to Ursula suggesting how Harry can manage his time more efficiently and answer these questions.

1 Why should Susana make the list of customers?

2 Which customers should Harry call first?

3 Why should he start visiting earlier?

4 Why should Harry keep sending information back?

5 Why should he divide up his area?

3 Language focus

Listen to Harry and Ursula again and complete the things they say.

HARRY: Over the next three months, (1) .... maintain sales of our services to current customers. (2) .... use the database to make a list of all the companies in my area ...
If I call them all next week, I can start visiting the following week.
(3) .... visit all the companies in the next two months.
(4) .... have time after that to go back and revisit the companies which are undecided.

URSULA: It's her job and she'll be much faster than you. (5) .... start calling your biggest customers ...
Keep sending the information you collect back to Susana.
(6) .... keep the database up-to-date,
(7) .... lose track of who you've visited and who you haven't visited. And one last thing: (8) .... divide up your area and concentrate your visits in smaller areas,
(9) .... find you're using your time more effectively ...

LANGUAGE FILE 1 >> PAGE 101

4 Communication activity

a Work in pairs. You work for a company that manufactures computer printers. Your company wants to launch an updated version of its bestselling printer, with some additional features. Decide on a schedule for a marketing campaign for the next six months. Decide on:

- overall goal of the schedule
- type of market research
- how to contact existing customers
- how to contact new customers
- ways of marketing (media, representatives, special offers ...)

b Explain your plans to another pair and listen to their plans. Discuss the good and bad points in your plans.

1 Vocabulary

Replace the words in italics in the sentences below with the correct form of these phrasal verbs.

catch up	come up	cut down	head off	hold up	put off

1 OK, I'm going to *leave* now. Bye!

2 Late deliveries from that new supplier have really *delayed* this project.

3 The company plans to *reduce* its spending by 5% next year.

4 Sorry, I have to go. A problem has *happened unexpectedly* at the office.

5 They'll have to *change* the meeting *to a later date*.

6 I'm working late today, *getting up-to-date* with my work.

VOCABULARY FILE 2 >> **PAGE 103**

2 Listening

a Dave Barton phones Nancy Dupont at Joly to discuss a future visit. Listen to the beginning of the conversation and answer these questions.

1 When is Dave visiting Joly?

2 Why is he calling?

b Listen to the rest of their conversation and note the changes they make on the schedule below.

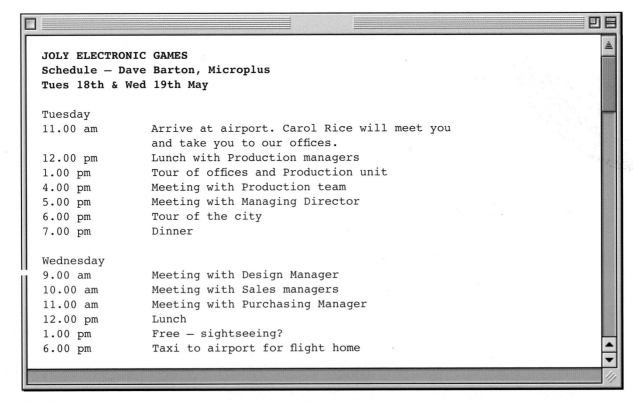

```
JOLY ELECTRONIC GAMES
Schedule — Dave Barton, Microplus
Tues 18th & Wed 19th May

Tuesday
11.00 am          Arrive at airport. Carol Rice will meet you
                  and take you to our offices.
12.00 pm          Lunch with Production managers
1.00 pm           Tour of offices and Production unit
4.00 pm           Meeting with Production team
5.00 pm           Meeting with Managing Director
6.00 pm           Tour of the city
7.00 pm           Dinner

Wednesday
9.00 am           Meeting with Design Manager
10.00 am          Meeting with Sales managers
11.00 am          Meeting with Purchasing Manager
12.00 pm          Lunch
1.00 pm           Free — sightseeing?
6.00 pm           Taxi to airport for flight home
```

③ Language focus

Match the halves to complete the things that Dave said in 2 Listening.

1 I was wondering if we	a cut down the tour?
2 Would it be possible	b that in the afternoon.
3 Do you think we could	c to put lunch back an hour?
4 I wonder if we could do	d could make some small changes.

LANGUAGE FILE 2 >> PAGE 102

④ Communication activity

STUDENT A: **Look at the information on page 79.**
STUDENT B: **Look at the information below.**

You are a supplier. Student A is a possible new customer who is coming to visit your company for two days. Student A will call you. Discuss this schedule for the visit. You want to keep your customer fairly busy so he/she doesn't have too much time to visit your competitors! But you want him/her to have an enjoyable visit which is not too busy.

Wednesday		**Thursday**	
10.30	Arrive. Coffee with senior management	9.00	Meeting with Purchasing Manager
11.30	Tour of factory and offices	10.30	Meeting with Production Manager
1.00	Lunch with Sales and Marketing teams	11.30	Meeting with Design team
2.00	Meeting with Marketing Manager	1.00	Lunch with Design and Production teams
4.00	Meeting with Sales Manager	2.00	Meeting – negotiations with senior management
5.00	Tour of city	4.00	Taxi to station for train home
7.00	Dinner		

**HOW'S YOUR
TIME MANAGEMENT?**

0–4 points:	Oh dear! You need to improve your time management – stop doing quizzes!
5–8 points:	Not too bad, but you can still manage your time better.
9–12 points:	Well done! You are doing OK.
13–16 points:	Superhuman! Are you sure you are telling the truth?

Vocabulary 1

Complete the puzzle.

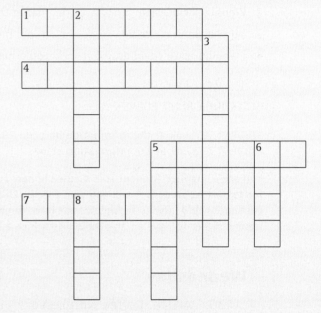

Across

1 You can place your order online – just visit our company ....

4 A type of menu that appears when you click on a small arrow.

5 Please .... to the bottom of this page to view our terms and conditions.

7 The opening page of a website.

Down

2 Are you looking for the perfect present? .... our online store for gift ideas.

3 The network of computers around the world which are used to exchange information.

5 If you know exactly what you want, just click here to .... for it.

6 Click on this .... to go to a page with related products.

8 A list of things to choose from.

Language 1

Choose the correct words in these sentences.

1 Have you heard the *last / latest* news about Linkit?

2 Did you *hear / heard* about the takeover of MLT?

3 Hey, that's *interesting / interested* news.

4 *What's / What* about her?

5 The article *writes / says* that DLS is going to close.

6 *I've / I'm* heard that Gill Bates is going to retire this year.

7 *Truly? / Really?* Where did you hear that?

8 That *surprises / surprise* me, actually.

Communication 1

Work in pairs. Tell each other about a website you use a lot for your work or studies.

• Describe the website.

• Say why you use it.

• Say what you like about it.

• Say what you don't like about it.

Vocabulary 2

Choose the two phrases in italics which go with the verb on the left.

1 keep *up-to-date | extra time | an appointment*

2 keep something *a deadline | on track | up-to-date*

3 lose *track | time | behind schedule*

4 make *a suggestion | a list | on time*

5 miss *an appointment | on track | a deadline*

6 put in *behind | extra time | more hours*

7 run *a list | behind schedule | on time*

Language 2

a Complete the sentences below with these words.

missed	expand	getting	follow	mean
go	recap	saying	think	decide

1 I'm afraid I don't .... what you're saying.

2 Can you .... on that? I think we need more details.

3 Shall we .... over what we've agreed?

4 I don't understand what you're .... at.

5 So, first of all, we need to .... who can do this.

6 We've discussed a lot, so I'd just like to .... the main points.

7 Sorry, I .... the second point.

8 That's a good point, but I .... we should open more branches.

9 What exactly do you .... by 'integrated structures'?

10 So, you're .... that we can double sales in a year.

Communication 2

a Work in pairs. Your company has a new director, who is going to visit your branch for the first time, for one day. Write a schedule for the day.

b Work with a different partner.

STUDENT A: Show your schedule for the day to Student B, the director, and discuss any necessary changes.

STUDENT B: You are the director. Look at Student A's schedule and ask for some changes to be made.

When you have finished, change roles and practise again with a different partner.

10 Advertising

UNIT GOALS ● understanding adverts ● using descriptive language ● talking about brands

TALKING POINT

Where do you see advertisements?

What kinds of advertisements do you like? Why?

How many brands can you name in 30 seconds?
   Make a list.

Why is branding important?

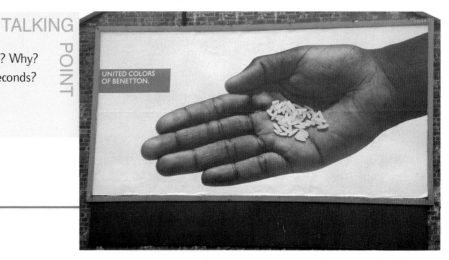

PART A Adverts

1 Vocabulary

a Match the adjectives 1–6 to the sentences a–f.

1	advanced	a	It looks smooth and shiny and has an attractive design.
2	affordable	b	It's complete and has everything you need.
3	sleek and stylish	c	This uses very new technology.
4	compatible	d	Most people can buy this because it's not too expensive.
5	comprehensive	e	It's not difficult to use.
6	easy-to-use	f	You can use it with different equipment.

b Work in pairs. Think of products you could describe using words from above.

VOCABULARY FILE >> PAGE 105

2 Reading

a Read the advertisements opposite and match them to these categories.

1 Entertainment   2 Communications   3 Travel

b Read the adverts again. Are these statements true (T) or false (F)?

1 Lufthansa's new Business Class is available on long-haul flights.

2 The airline's laptops are connected to the seats.

3 Your airline seat becomes a bed.

4 SMK televisions look good.

5 SMK televisions provide 12 months' guarantee.

6 It costs £50 to install a BT Business Broadband network.

7 Computers in the office can be networked in half an hour.

8 BT's service will change your business a lot.

a

Made to measure: our new Business Class for long-haul flights.

Regardless of whether you'd like to work, relax or sleep 10,000 metres in the air, our new Business Class is well-prepared. With an integrated laptop connection directly at the seat. With a comprehensive entertainment programme. And with an infinitely variable seat, which transforms at the push of a button into a new PrivateBed – the longest bed in its class. For reservations and further information, visit **www.lufthansa.com**

There's no better way to fly. Lufthansa. A Star Alliance member.

b

There's never been a better time to watch television.

That's because SMK now offers a range of affordable, compatible flat-screen televisions. They're sleek. They're stylish. And they make watching television more enjoyable than ever. There's also a 12-month guarantee, so what are you waiting for?

www.SMK.com/televisions ◑ **SMK**

c

Get your office networked in an hour.

Get £50 off if you apply now.

When you network your people together, you can get the full benefit of BT Business Broadband. With Office in an Hour, you can have the computers in your office networked wirelessly in just one hour. Apply online before 30th April and you can get £50 off our starter pack.

To find out more about how BT Broadband and IT applications can transform your business, call 0800 517 518. **BT**

bt.com/businessbroadband

3 Language focus

Complete the following sentences from the adverts in 2 Reading.

1 The .... bed in its class.

2 There's never been a .... time to watch television.

3 They make watching television .... than ever.

4 .... £50 off .... you .... now.

LANGUAGE FILE 1 >> PAGE 104

4 Communication activity

a Work in pairs. Choose one of these products and write an advertisement for it.

b Give your advert to another pair to read and comment on.

1 Listening

🔊 **Listen to Lisa Chen talking about her company, Multiform, and answer the questions.**

1 What is the standard package?

2 Why is it used by so many designers?

3 Why didn't Multiform need to use expensive advertising?

2 Language focus

🔊 **a Listen again and complete these things that Lisa said in** 1 Listening.

1 Multiform software .... its flexibility.

2 That's why it's .... professional designers.

3 Multiform .... being a complete all-in-one design package.

4 Multiform .... mainly by word of mouth.

🔊 **b Listen again and check.**

LANGUAGE FILE 2 >> PAGE 105

3 Exploring

a How many of these companies/brands do you know? What image do they have and how did they get it? In pairs, describe each company's image. Use these words and/or any other words you can think of.

| exciting | innovative | safe | high-class | long-lasting | reliable |

Reproduced with permission of YAHOO! INC. © 2000 by Yahoo! Inc.
YAHOO! and the YAHOO! logo are trademarks of Yahoo! Inc.

Example
Volvo is known for being safe.

b In pairs, talk about the image of your company or one that you know.

4 Culture focus

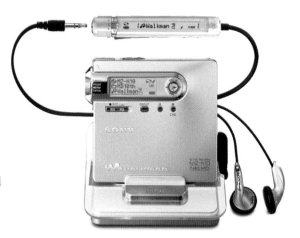

a Read the article and answer the questions.

1 When was the Walkman invented?

2 Who created the brand?

3 How did Sony launch the Walkman in Japan?

4 Why didn't Sony want to use the name 'Walkman' in other countries?

5 Why did the name 'Walkman' become commonly used around the world?

Walkman (*plural* **Walkmans**) /ˈwɔːk.mən/ us /ˈwaːk-/ *noun* [c] (*ALSO* **personal stereo**) *TRADEMARK* a small CASSETTE PLAYER, sometimes with radio, with small HEADPHONES

The story of Sony Walkman and its worldwide branding success

In 1979, an empire in personal portable entertainment was created. It began with the invention of the first cassette Walkman TPS-L2, which changed forever the way consumers listen to music. Since its introduction, the Walkman has been a product and marketing success. It took the world by storm as demand for the pocket-sized, 390 gram personal portable player rocketed beyond imagination.

The Walkman brand was created by staff at Sony and named by them. Sony promoted the product in an unconventional way by getting part-time student workers to wear and listen to their Walkman on trains, campuses and around the very busy Ginza district in Tokyo. This proved to be a great success.

When Walkman was ready for launch overseas, Sony in America did not approve of the name as it decided that 'Walkman' was not proper English. It therefore decided to launch under the different name of 'Soundabout'. Similarly it was renamed 'Stowaway' in the UK and called 'Freestyle' in Sweden. But many overseas visitors to Japan had heard about the latest innovation and were asking shop owners where they could purchase a Walkman. The Sony Walkman name had gone global before the product, and the term 'Walkman' quickly became a noun in the English language.

Worldwide shipments of all Sony Walkman products (cassette, compact disc and MiniDisc) have now passed 240 million.

b Work in pairs. What other global brands can you think of? Why are they so successful?

11 Trading

UNIT GOALS ● talking about different shipping methods ● taking and placing orders
● dealing with shipping problems

How do you send things to people …
… in your area?
… overseas?
What imports are popular in your country? What is exported?

PART A   Ordering

1 Vocabulary

a Work in pairs. Match the shipping methods to the photos.

1 sea freight

2 air freight

3 airmail

4 motorcycle messenger

5 courier

b Look at these situations. Decide which shipping method to use, and why.

1 A travel agency needs to get an airline ticket to a customer in the same city on the same day.

2 A new company in South Africa wants to import cars from the UK. The company is opening for business in six months.

3 A Polish company wants to order 1,000 books urgently from New York.

4 A Spanish company needs to send two T-shirts to a customer in Sweden.

5 An Irish company has a small package that needs to arrive in Germany tomorrow.

VOCABULARY FILE >> PAGE 107

2 Listening

a Match the words 1–4 to their meanings a–d.

1 purchase order number

2 order

3 shipping method

4 forwarder

a the items that the customer wants

b a company that transports goods or arranges transport

c the number that the customer gives the order

d the way that the order is transported

◁» **b** **Listen to a customer placing an order and complete the order form.**

Company: (1) .... Ltd.   Account no.: (5) ....
Shipping address: Unit (2) ....   Purchase order no.: (6) ....
            (3) .... Industrial Estate   Order: (7) .... x item no. (8) ....
            (4) .... Avenue   Shipping method: (9) ....
            Pickford   Forwarder: (10) .... Forwarding

3 Language focus

a **Match the halves to make complete questions from** 2 Listening.

1 Can I just take some   a forwarder you want us to use?

2 Could I have your company   b confirm the shipping address for me?

3 Can you give me   c name and account number?

4 Could you tell   d details from you?

5 Can I check which shipping   e your purchase order number?

6 Would you   f me what shipping method you'd like to use?

◁» **b** **Listen again and check.**

LANGUAGE FILE 1 >> PAGE 106

4 Communication activity

STUDENT A: **Look at the information on page 81.**
STUDENT B: **Look at the information below.**

Situation 1
You are a customer. Use the information below to place an order with Student A. Call Student A and give the necessary details.

Company: *Masters Trading*
Shipping address: *Real 209*
                   Salamanca
                   Spain
Account no.:   *1097004*
Purchase order no.: *AF1782*
Order: *10 x item no. 783296*
                   5 x item no. 783971
Shipping method: *Air freight*
Forwarder: *Heathrow Freight Services*

Situation 2
You work for a shipping company. Student A will call you to place an order. Ask questions to make sure you get all the details you need to complete the form.

Company: ....
Shipping address: ....
....
Account no.: ....
Purchase order no.: ....
Order: ....
Shipping method: ....
Forwarder: ....

5 Writing

You work for a shipping company. A customer placed an order with you by email, but forgot to provide you with the following information:

• shipping address   • preferred shipping method   • the name of the forwarder

Write an email asking for the information you need.

1 Reading

a   **Work in pairs. Discuss which three of these things are most important in a delivery company.**

- delivery on time
- friendly delivery staff
- delivery with no damaged goods
- friendly staff on the phone
- delivery of the right goods

b   **Read this case study and answer the questions.**

1   Was the supplier pleased with the results of the survey?

2   What was the most important thing for the supplier?

3   Was it the same for the customer?

4   What did the supplier do as a result?

Are you really giving your customers what they want?

Company X carried out a survey of its major customers. It was horrified to learn that one of its most important customers had given a low score for reliable delivery, while ranking this requirement very highly.

The Sales Director spoke to the Production Manager, who produced a record of 100% on-time delivery. The Sales Director was puzzled. He spoke to the customer to clarify the situation, and was told that on-time delivery was not the customer's measure of overall delivery reliability, and that 30% of orders were incomplete, incorrect or contained damaged items.

From this situation, Company X learned that it was measuring the wrong things – what was important to the company was not the most important thing to the customer. It changed its system to ensure that it checked the things that really mattered to its customers.

2 Listening

a **Listen to three conversations about shipping problems. Match each conversation to one of the problems a–c.**

a Only part of the order has arrived.

b Some items are damaged.

c The customer hasn't received the order.

b **Listen again and complete the table.**

	Order number	Items ordered	When shipped
1			
2			
3			

3 Language focus

Complete the sentences below from 2 Listening **with these words.**

apologize	arrange	arrived	expecting
ordered	received	Due	sorry	change

Complaint

1 I'm .... an order of 150 tables, but it hasn't .... yet.

2 We .... 130 jackets, but we've only .... 100.

Apology

3 I'm .... you haven't received it.

4 I do ....

Explanation

5 .... to low stock levels, we could only ship 100 last week.

Action

6 I'll .... an urgent delivery by courier.

7 There'll be no shipping .... for that, of course.

LANGUAGE FILE 2 >> PAGE 106

4 Communication activity

STUDENT A: **Look at the information on page 81.**
STUDENT B: **Look at the information below.**

You are a customer. Call Student A about two orders.

Situation 1
You ordered 50 modems by air freight with purchase order number 987235. You need them by next week.

Situation 2
You have received your order of 1,000 T-shirts, but one case was open so 50 T-shirts are wet and dirty.

Now change roles. Student A, a customer, will call you to ask about two orders.

Situation 3
Some titles were temporarily out of stock. Apologize. You will send them soon.

Situation 4
Apologize and offer collection and replacement.

12 Reporting

UNIT GOALS • summarizing written information • writing reports

What kind of written information do people summarize?
What are the benefits of summarizing?
What kinds of reports do you have to read or write ...
    ... in your language?
    ... in English?

PART A Summaries

1 Listening

a You are going to listen to an interview with a business trainer, about writing summaries. Work in pairs. Read the interviewer's questions and discuss possible answers.

1 What's the first step in writing a summary?

2 And what's the second stage?

3 What about charts and graphs? Should you just copy them into your summary?

4 How do you decide what information to put in and what to leave out?

5 What should you check when reading through your summary?

b Listen to the interview and write the trainer's answers.

c Are the answers the same as yours? Do you agree with the advice given?

2 Reading

You work for a computer consultancy firm which has been asked to assess the computing needs of another company, Adline. Read the report opposite about Adline and complete the timeline below with the key stages.

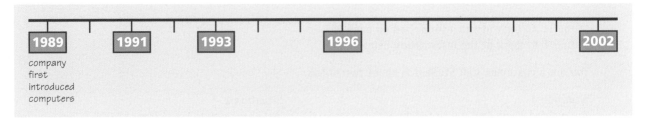

1989 — company first introduced computers
1991
1993
1996
2002

The development of computers at Adline

The company first introduced computers for all its employees in 1989. At that time, there was a lot of resistance from employees, as they had either been using typewriters, in the case of secretarial staff for example, or other similar methods which could be described as part-manual, part-automated.

There was no real consultation with staff about the introduction of computers; it was largely imposed, as the company knew it had to do this to become more efficient. However, there was an extensive training programme in place before the computers were introduced, and ongoing support during the transition period. Gradually, most employees came to like the new computer systems. In 1991, the company's computers were linked to each other for the first time in a network. There were some problems at first, which led to a certain amount of employee frustration, but these were overcome fairly quickly.

In 1993, a completely new computer network was installed, using the Windows operating system for the first time. Managers were concerned that staff would not be happy with a second big change in less than three years, but in fact this was well received, as employees quickly came to prefer Windows to the old DOS-based system.

In 1996, all computers gained permanent access to the Internet and email. Again, this was well received by employees once initial problems were ironed out. But in the following years, employees became more unhappy with email in particular, as they felt it was starting to replace face-to-face contact with managers and fellow employees. In 2002, broadband Internet was introduced throughout the company, which everyone is pleased with, mainly because it allows email attachments to be sent and received much more quickly.

Language focus

Your manager has asked you to prepare a summary of Adline's computing needs. Read the report again and highlight the key information.

LANGUAGE FILE 1 >> **PAGE 107**

Writing

a Work in pairs. Write a summary of the Adline report in 2 Reading, based on the key information.

b Work with another pair. Read each other's summaries and compare them. Are there any differences? Can you make any improvements?

1 Vocabulary

Put the phrases below into the correct columns.

go up a lot	go up a bit	go down a lot	go down a bit	no change

decrease slightly　　　nosedive　　　increase slightly　　　stay the same

fall sharply　　　rise a little　　　rise sharply　　　rocket

increase dramatically　　　remain steady　　　plummet　　　dive

shoot up　　　decrease dramatically　　　fall a little

VOCABULARY FILE >> PAGE 108

2 Reading

a　Work in pairs. What do you think *e-readiness* is?

b　Read the report below about e-readiness and decide if these statements are true (T) or false (F).

1　e-readiness is an assessment of how many people use the Internet.

2　There is a new EIU ranking every year.

3　The EIU only assesses the countries' technology.

4　The US is always ranked first.

5　In Scandinavia, people's lives have changed a lot because of the Internet.

6　Most countries in the ranking are progressing in e-readiness.

EIU e-readiness rankings 2000–2004

'e-readiness' is a measure of whether a country is in a good position to increase Internet-based business. The Economist Intelligence Unit (EIU) publishes an annual e-readiness ranking of the world's 60 largest economies.

The EIU assesses countries' technology infrastructure, their general business environment, the number of e-business transactions taking place, social and cultural conditions that influence Internet usage, and the availability of support for e-businesses.

The ranking was started in 2000, and the US was then the world leader. Canada and Australia were also in strong positions, but they have dropped a little each year as other countries have risen, especially in Northern Europe. In 2003, the US was overtaken by Sweden and, in 2004, the US fell sharply to sixth place, below Denmark, the UK, Sweden, Norway and Finland.

The US is still making progress in e-readiness, but other countries are making faster progress. High-speed Internet access and advanced e-business services are increasing rapidly in Northern Europe. Scandinavian citizens in particular have incorporated Internet technology into their daily lives, changing how they work, shop and communicate with officials.

Denmark (1st) and South Korea (14th) have risen very sharply in the last five years. Some countries have fallen dramatically in the same period, for example, Australia, Egypt, Japan, Peru and Russia. However, they are not doing badly – nearly every country in the ranking is making progress, but some are progressing more quickly than others.

3 Language focus

a Match these verb forms to the examples below from the report in 2 Reading.

Past simple   Present continuous   Passive   Present perfect

a ....

They **have dropped** a little each year.

Some countries **have fallen** dramatically.

c ....

The ranking **was started** in 2000.

In 2003, the US **was overtaken** by Sweden.

b ....

Canada and Australia **were** also in strong positions.

In 2004, the US **fell** sharply.

d ....

The US **is** still **making** progress.

Some **are progressing** more quickly than others.

b Match these explanations to the verb forms above.

1 It makes the report less personal and more formal.

2 It describes recent changes.

3 It describes events at the moment.

4 It describes events that happened in the past.

LANGUAGE FILE 2 >> **PAGE 108**

4 Communication activity

STUDENT A: **Look at the information on page 81.**
STUDENT B: **Look at the information below.**

Look at the information about mobile phone ownership in the UK for 2001 and 2003. Answer Student A's questions. Ask Student A questions so you can complete the chart with information for the last six columns for 2001.

Example

B: *What percentage of people between 15 and 24 years old owned mobile phones in 2001?*

A: *Just over 80%.*

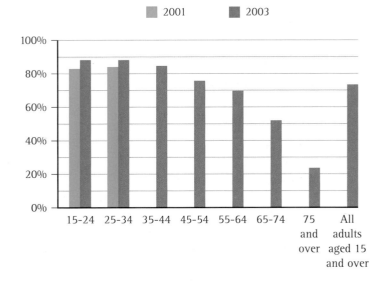

Adult mobile phone ownership by age, 2001 and 2003

5 Writing

a Work in pairs. Write a report on trends in mobile phone ownership. Decide which are the most important trends, based on the information in the graphs in 4 Communication activity.

b Work with another pair. Read each other's reports and compare them. Are there any differences? Can you make improvements?

Vocabulary 1

Complete the puzzle.

Across

1 Including everything.

7 Using the latest technology.

8 Useable in different situations.

9 Looks smooth and shiny.

Down

1 A .... sofa is nice to sit in.

2 Doesn't cost much to operate.

3 Attractive and fashionable.

4 Not expensive to buy.

5 'This software is .... with all operating systems.'

6 Easy to carry around.

Language 1

Choose the correct words in these sentences.

There are other laptops that are more affordable (1) *that / than* the CPQ, but the CPQ is definitely the (2) *better / best* value for money in its class. It's also (3) *more easy / easier* to use than any of the others, and it's the (4) *sleekest / most sleek* model on the market at the moment. It's the (5) *flexiblest / most flexible* laptop you will find, and although it's (6) *the heaviest / the heavyest* model available, it is (7) *more portable / most portable* than any of the others, because of its well-designed case – the (8) *more stylish / most stylish* case that I have ever seen.

Communication 1

Work in pairs.

Situation 1

STUDENT A: You work for an office furniture supplier. Student B is going to call you to place an order. Prepare the questions you will need to ask. When you are both ready, role play the conversation.

STUDENT B: You are going to call Student A to place an order for some office furniture. Think about what you want to order, and what details you will have to give. When you are both ready, role play the conversation.

Situation 2

STUDENT A: You are going to call Student B to place an order for some office equipment. Think about what you want to order, and what details you will have to give. When you are both ready, role play the conversation.

STUDENT B: You work for an office equipment supplier. Student A is going to call you to place an order. Prepare the questions you will need to ask. When you are both ready, role play the conversation.

Vocabulary 2

Look at this table comparing a country's economy in 2004 and 2005. Match the sentence halves below to make complete sentences which describe the information in the table.

	2004	2005
Average salary	€40,000	€45,000
Average house price	€150,000	€250,000
Income tax	20%	19.75%
Interest rate	4%	4%
Unemployment	3.5% of population	1% of population

1 The average salary	a stayed the same.
2 The average house price	b plummeted.
3 Income tax	c shot up.
4 The interest rate	d increased a little.
5 Unemployment	e fell slightly.

Language 2

Work in pairs. Discuss these sentences. In each pair, what verb forms are used? What is the difference in meaning between each sentence?

1a It is predicted that sales will increase a lot in the next six months.

 b Chris Worth and Steve Dwyer predict that sales will increase a lot in the next six months.

2a This system was introduced in 2003.

 b The Director introduced this system in 2003.

3a Sales have fallen dramatically in the last two years.

 b Sales fell dramatically between 2002 and 2004.

4a The design changes have improved the product and increased sales.

 b The design changes improved the product and increased sales.

5a KPLG imports a lot of components from Sweden.

 b KPLG is importing a lot of components from Sweden.

Communication 2

Work in pairs.

Situation 1

STUDENT A: You work for a computer software wholesaler. Student B is going to call you about a problem with an order. Think about what to say. When you are both ready, role play the conversation.

STUDENT B: You work for a computer shop. You recently received a delivery of computer software from Student A's company, but there were some problems with it. You are going to call Student A. Think about what to say. When you are both ready, role play the conversation.

Situation 2

STUDENT A: You work for a clothes shop. You recently received a delivery of clothes from Student B's company, but there were some problems with it. You are going to call Student B. Think about what to say. When you are both ready, role play the conversation.

STUDENT B: You work for a clothes manufacturer. Student A is going to call you about a problem with an order. Think about what to say. When you are both ready, role play the conversation.

13 Presentations

UNIT GOALS ● listening to a presentation ● giving a presentation

TALKING POINT

What makes a good presentation?

Have you been to presentations …

    … in your language?

    … in English?

Have you ever given a presentation …

    … in your language?

    … in English?

PART A Attending presentations

1 Vocabulary

a **Put these parts of a presentation in the order you would hear them.**

a Summarizing

b Introducing

c Closing

d Welcoming

e Moving from point to point

b **Match these expressions to the parts of a presentation above. There are two expressions for each part.**

1 Are there any questions?

2 Good morning, everyone.

3 To sum up …

4 Welcome to …

5 Thank you for listening.

6 That brings me to my next point.

7 Today you're going to listen to …

8 I'll start the presentation by … then I'll go on to … and I'll finish with …

9 To summarize …

10 I'd like to move on now, to look at …

2 Listening

🔊 **Listen to the beginning of a presentation by Tim Harman, from Mallory Products, on the subject of branding. What are the three main parts of the presentation?**

3 Language focus

Listen to some comments and questions at the end of Tim's presentation and complete the sentences.

1 First, ... I think your ideas are excellent.

2 You .... this model might not be practical for all types of brands.

3 Could you .... a brand where it might not work so well?

4 I'm not sure .... about losing market position.

5 Could you .... why that happened?

6 One thing ....: 'Brand loyalty is often overestimated.'

7 Can I just .... by that?

LANGUAGE FILE 1 >> **PAGE 109**

4 Communication activity

STUDENT A: Look at the information on page 82.
STUDENT B: Look at the information below.

a You work in Marketing for a large chain of music stores. Prepare a short presentation on recent trends in sales of music CD singles, based on the information in the graph.

Use these notes to help you. Use some, but not all, of the information from the main part.

Introduction
Your name, company name, type of company, topic of presentation.

Main part
Singles traditionally cheap, teenagers liked to have them in their music collection. Now more expensive, not very good value.

Recent technology – different ways to buy and listen to music; competition from DVD, MiniDisc, MP3, Inernet downloads, so not necessary to buy CDs from shops.

Teenagers prefer cheaper, more 'high-tech' ways of getting music.

Summary
Need to make CD singles cheaper.

Need to find new ways to market CD singles.

Need to think about moving into Internet music more.

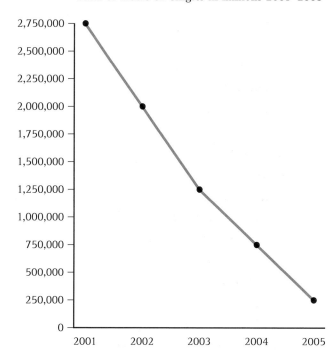

Sales of music CD singles in millions 2001–2005

b Listen to Student A's presentation and make notes. When he/she has finished, ask some questions.

Ask Student A ...

... why something happened

... to clarify something

... to explain something again

... to give an example of something

c Give your presentation to Student A. When you have finished, answer Student A's questions.

1 Reading

a **Work in pairs. What advice would you give someone who is going to give a presentation? Think about:**

- eye contact
- voice
- body language

b **Read the article from a business magazine about giving presentations. Compare your answers in (a) with the advice in the text.**

Eye contact

You can communicate a lot through eye contact. To establish rapport with each member of your audience and make them feel you are talking to them, try to make eye contact regularly. During your talk, hold your gaze for five or six seconds at a time in different directions.

Voice

The simple advice is to slow down and take your time. You will not normally be interrupted, so you can pause. Make sure you are loud enough so that everyone can hear. Monitor the audience to check that they can hear you. Try to vary the pitch of your voice. A monotone speech is very boring.

Body language

The way you stand conveys a great deal about you. Stand up straight and try to look alert and interested. What to do with your hands is always a problem. They must not wave aimlessly through the air, or fiddle with a pen, or remain in your pockets. Find a safe resting place. Return your hands there after a gesture is complete.

2 Listening

Listen to three extracts from Tim Harman's presentation and choose the correct words in italics.

Extract 1

1 Tim's company has to maintain *one leading brand | several leading brands*.

2 Glimmer was the *biggest | second biggest* seller in its market.

3 In 2004, sales of Glimmer went *up | down*.

Extract 2

4 The company is *happy | unhappy* with sales of Glimmer now.

5 Tim thinks Glimmer is a *good | bad* example for other businesses to follow.

Extract 3

6 Tim would like to hear comments from *customers who try his products | companies who try his methods*.

3 Language focus

a **Complete the sentences below, from different parts of Tim's presentation, with the words in the box.**

> summarize   start   shows   remind   questions
>
> end   could   called   brings

1 And just to .... you, my presentation today is .... 'Keeping it Going: Maintaining a Successful Brand'.

2 I'll .... by discussing what exactly we mean by 'branding'.

3 And that .... me to the second and central part of my talk.

4 This graph .... the kinds of sales figures it had.

5 I .... say a lot more about that, but now I'd like to explain ...

6 So, to ...., we started off by looking at what a brand is, then ...

7 And that brings me to the .... of this presentation.

8 Does anyone have any ....?

b **Listen and check.**

LANGUAGE FILE 2 >> **PAGE 110**

4 Communication activity

a **Prepare a short presentation (maximum five minutes) on one of these topics, or choose one of your own.**

- a work/college project you are working on at the moment
- a work/college procedure or system
- a piece of equipment
- a plan

Use these headings to help you:

- Welcome and introduction
- Main points
- Summary
- Close and questions

b **Work in small groups. Take turns to give your presentations to the group. After you have listened to the others' presentations, ask questions.**

14 | Companies

UNIT GOALS ● talking about companies ● talking about organizational culture

What kind of company do you work for,
or would you like to work for?
What different kinds of companies are there?

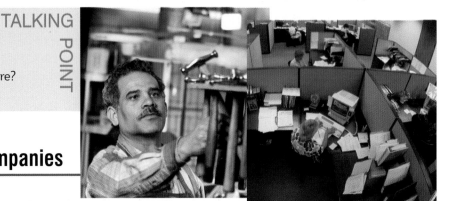

PART A Different companies

1 Reading

Read about four companies below and complete the table.

	Type of company	Where is it based?	What field is it in?	How is it managed?
1 Rank Group plc				
2 Edinburgh Bicycle Co-operative				
3 Graphic Plus				
4 Oxfam				

1

The Rank Group plc is a UK-based public limited company, with shareholders all around the world. It is run by a board of directors with six directors, and five committees managing different aspects of the business, which focuses on leisure and entertainment.

2

EDINBURGHBICYCLECOOPERATIVE

Edinburgh Bicycle Co-operative is a chain of bicycle shops in Scotland and Northern England. Every full-time worker becomes a member of the co-operative after one year, with an equal share in the business and its profits. There are currently 40 co-operative members running the business.

3

Graphic Plus is a design company based in Bristol in the UK. It is a limited company with three directors and sixteen employees. The company encourages creativity and innovation, and there are weekly meetings to discuss everything from design ideas to suggestions about the way the company is run.

4

Oxfam GB is an international charity set up to fight poverty and suffering. It is run by a Council of Trustees, with between 10 and 12 members, and operates as a company limited by guarantee. It has about 700 paid employees at its headquarters in Oxford, and about 2,000 others around the world. It also has over 20,000 volunteers working in the UK, mainly in its shops.

Oxfam

2 Vocabulary

Find words in the texts in 1 Reading **which mean:**

1 investors who own a small part of a company (text 1)

2 a group of people who manage a company (text 1)

3 a company which is owned and managed equally by all its employees (text 2)

4 the money which a company makes, after paying all its costs (text 2)

5 a company that the public cannot buy parts of (text 3)

6 an organization whose main aim is social, not financial (text 4)

7 people who manage a charity (text 4)

8 people who work without receiving a salary (text 4)

VOCABULARY FILE >> PAGE 112

3 Listening

Listen to a conversation at a conference between Amy and Geoff and decide if these statements are true (T) or false (F).

1 Geoff works for ALC.

2 Amy works for ALC.

3 Amy's company provides leisure services for the public.

4 ALC owns some fitness clubs.

5 ALC helps companies to increase their business.

6 Amy specializes in market research.

7 ALC often has to suggest big changes.

8 Geoff's company is in a similar field.

4 Language focus

a **Complete the things which Amy and Geoff said in** 3 Listening **with these words and phrases.**

provide	aim to	to develop	come up with
involve	in charge of	deal with	offer

1 What does that ....?

2 Well, basically, we .... help organizations ...

3 We .... a complete diagnosis and solution package.

4 We .... a wide range of organizations.

5 We .... a service tailored to the client.

6 My department's .... the market research side of things.

7 And then you try and .... solutions?

8 We try .... a plan.

b **Listen again and check.**

LANGUAGE FILE 1 >> PAGE 111

5 Communication activity

STUDENT A: **Look at the information on page 80.**
STUDENT B: **Look at the information on page 83.**

1 Listening

Listen to Rob Carter talking about the organizational culture of Apex Advertising and complete the sentences with the words he uses.

1 For us, organizational culture is the way people in the organization ...., behave and ....

2 It influences .... at every level.

3 We have worked for years to develop a culture focused on .... and ....

4 Everyone feels like .... team.

5 Our workplace is ...., with nobody working behind closed doors.

2 Reading

a **Quickly read the Co-operative Group's Statement of Principles opposite to find the answers to these questions.**

the Co-operative Group

1 What part of the Group is most familiar to the public?

2 Is the Group good to work for?

b **Read the text again and match the headings to the paragraphs.**

a ... to the wider world

b ... to the environment

c ... to the community

d ... to our employees

e ... to quality and value for money

f ... to serve everyone

g ... to provide accurate information and to respect our customers' rights

h ... to provide a high-quality service

c **Work in pairs. Decide which three of the Co-op's commitments are most important, and why. Compare with another pair and discuss any differences.**

3 Language focus

Match the halves to make sentences from 2 Reading.

1 We aim	a offering comprehensive training ...
2 We seek to	b is wrong for many of the world's citizens ...
3 We recognize that all	c offer a friendly, courteous and efficient service.
4 We are committed to	d to deliver a quality service to customers.
5 The Co-op believes that it	e commercial activity has an impact ...

LANGUAGE FILE 2 >> PAGE 111

4 Communication activity

STUDENT A: **Look at the information on page 79.**
STUDENT B: **Look at the information on page 83.**

The Co-operative Group Statement of Principles

The Co-operative Group is one of the largest consumer co-operative organizations in the world. It is owned by its members, and operates across numerous business fields – including retail, travel, funerals, insurance and banking. It is best known for its retail operation, which consists of 1,600 stores, from convenience stores to supermarkets and department stores. Together, they account for over 25% of all co-operative retail trade in the UK. We aim to deliver a quality service to customers, and to contribute to the well-being and enrichment of society, through good operating practices and by re-investing our profits in our business and in the communities we serve.

Our commitment ...

1

We aim to cater for the needs of the young, the old, those with disabilities, busy families; in fact to serve the whole community.

2

We seek to offer a friendly, courteous and efficient service to all our customers.

3

We offer good-quality products at fair prices, and all our grocery products are backed by our unique guarantee.

4

We will always aim to adhere scrupulously to all laws designed to protect the customer, and to describe our goods and services accurately, giving as much information about them as we can. We will campaign to secure further legal safeguards wherever we believe the consumer is vulnerable in order to raise standards of protection for all.

5

We recognize that all commercial activity has an impact on the environment, but we are determined to measure and to minimize the adverse effects of our activities while positively contributing to environmental improvement.

6

Retailing is a business about people. We are committed to offering comprehensive training and good terms and conditions for all our employees.

7

The Co-op is part of the community and actively contributes to the well-being of the communities it serves.

8

The Co-op believes that it is wrong for many of the world's citizens to be condemned to a life of poverty and, while recognizing the limitations of its influence, will seek, whenever it can, to ensure that producers in developing countries get a fair reward for their efforts.

UNIT
15 | Changes at work

UNIT GOALS • talking about changes at work • talking about working conditions

TALKING POINT

What changes can happen to a company?
What changes have you seen in your company or college,
or in any companies that you know?
How have working conditions improved in recent years?

PART A   Company changes

1 Vocabulary

Match the words 1–6 to their meanings a–f.

1	acquisition/takeover	a	major changes in the way a company is organized
2	relocation	b	two different companies agree to work closely together
3	merger	c	the workplace moves to a different place
4	diversification	d	two different companies become one company
5	restructuring	e	one company buys another company
6	joint venture	f	a company starts to operate in different fields

VOCABULARY FILE 1 >> PAGE 114

2 Listening

a Listen to Louise, a senior manager, talking to employees about a company merger. Complete the three things that she tells them.

1 Nobody will ....

2 Some of our operations ....

3 There will be some ....

b Listen to Louise answering employees' questions about the merger and decide if these statements are true (T) or false (F).

1 There will probably be no job losses for five years.

2 After the relocation, nobody will have a longer journey to work.

3 Mackenzie will provide staff training if it is needed.

4 Employees will earn less working for the new merged company.

3 Language focus

a **Complete the sentences below, which Louise said in** 2 Listening, **with these words.**

reassure	update	far	picture	idea	keep	
know	development					

1 We want to .... you in the
   ....

2 I've been asked to .... you with three
   pieces of news.

3 I can .... you that nobody will lose their job.

4 There has been a new .... regarding
   restructuring plans.

5 Just to give you an ...., you may find that your job title changes slightly.

6 As .... as I ...., we're hoping for a five-year guarantee on job security.

b **Complete the questions below from** 2 Listening **with these words.**

affect	mean (x2)	happen

1 Does that .... our jobs are completely secure forever?

2 How will the relocation .... us?

3 What will .... if our job changes a lot because of all the department changes?

4 What does it .... for our salaries?

LANGUAGE FILE 1 >> PAGE 113

4 Communication activity

STUDENT A: **Look at the information on page 83.**
STUDENT B: **Look at the information below.**

Situation 1
You are the manager of a medium-sized business which is going to be taken over by a larger multinational company. Tell Student A, one of your employees, about the probable changes:

• relocation of offices to another site in the city

• some employees working abroad

• more responsibilities for some employees

Answer Student A's questions.

Situation 2
You work for a medium-sized business which is going to be taken over by a larger multinational company. Listen to Student A, your manager, tell you about probable changes. You have a young family and are concerned about these changes. Ask questions to find out more about them.

PART B Working conditions

1 Vocabulary

Complete the sentences below with these words.

flexible hours	holiday	maternity leave	unpaid leave
pension	sick leave	paternity leave	

1 I get six weeks' annual paid ...., so I can have a really good break from work whenever I need it.

2 I don't have to worry about money if I'm ill, because I can take up to 26 weeks' paid .... a year.

3 My employer was very good when I wanted to go travelling around the world – he gave me six months' .... and kept my job open for me.

4 My wife's having a baby soon, so she's on .... now. When the baby's born, I'll get four weeks ...., too.

5 I won't have to worry about money when I retire – I'm in a very good company .... scheme.

6 The company I work for offers ...., which is great for me as I have young children at school.

VOCABULARY FILE 2 >> PAGE 115

2 Reading

Read the text below about employment laws in Europe and complete it with these headings.

a Anti-discrimination
b Conditions of work
c Parental leave
d Pay
e Notice of termination
f Time off for other reasons

The European Union

The European Union (EU) has a long tradition of ensuring a decent working environment for all throughout the EU and of protecting workers' rights. This is done by agreeing common minimum rules on working conditions and health and safety at work, and by promoting modern labour relations and dialogue between worker representatives and employers. Although working conditions are similar across the EU, there are of course national and cultural differences between different countries.

1 .... All employees have the right to work in a safe and secure environment, up to a maximum number of hours per day/week, and with some time off for holidays.

2 .... Everyone should earn at least the national minimum wage, depending on their age. They should receive a document explaining their wages, and employers should only take away necessary taxes, insurance and pension payments.

3 .... Employers must give a reason for dismissing an employee, and give a minimum period of notice to the employee. They must not dismiss an employee without good reason.

4 .... Women who are going to have a baby have the right to take time off work before and after the birth. They should receive payments for at least some of this period. Fathers also have the right to take leave at the time of the birth and afterwards, although they may not receive payment for this.

5 .... Employees can take time off work for family emergencies or some official duties, but the employer does not have to pay them for this.

6 .... Employers must offer the same opportunities to both men and women, and pay them the same wage for the same job. They must take all possible reasonable measures to ensure that disabled employees can perform the same tasks as others.

3 Listening

a Listen to three managers talking about changes in working conditions and complete the table.

	What has changed?	Does the manager think the change is positive?
1		
2		
3		

b Listen again and choose the best answers.

Speaker 1

1 Employees no longer worry about:
   a their families
   b finishing a job

2 Employees are now:
   a less stressed
   b more challenged at work

3 The changes have:
   a reduced costs
   b increased costs

Speaker 2

4 Men:
   a fall asleep at their desks nowadays
   b fell asleep at their desks in the past

5 Some male employees:
   a want special training for fathers
   b don't intend to become a father

6 These should be a system of:
   a baby leave
   b family leave

Speaker 3

7 Part-time workers used to:
   a take too much sick leave
   b become ill from working too much

8 The recent change has:
   a cost the company a lot
   b not cost the company a lot

9 The company has:
   a put prices up for customers
   b reduced prices to customers

4 Language focus

Match the halves to make complete sentences from 3 Listening.

1 As a result
2 Because of
3 A consequence
4 It means
5 But it has
6 As a
7 Consequently,
8 This has resulted

a caused bad feeling among some of the male employees.
b in cost-cutting in other areas.
c of new legislation, everyone's working week was reduced.
d of that is happier employees.
e part-time workers don't make themselves ill.
f that men don't fall asleep at their desks.
g this, employees are spending more time with their family.
h result, everyone can afford to take some time off.

LANGUAGE FILE 2 >> PAGE 115

5 Exploring

Work in groups. Look at these changes in working conditions that have taken place in recent years. Do you think they are all positive? What effects have they had on employees, managers and companies?

- shorter more flexible working hours
- longer holidays
- longer maternity and paternity leave
- more private pension schemes
- better conditions for part-time and temporary staff
- more equality in the workplace

Vocabulary 1

a   Find 11 words in the puzzle that are related to companies.

L	I	A	F	O	S	H	A	P	R	I	V	Z
I	C	Q	K	S	H	O	N	R	U	T	W	E
M	V	D	O	N	A	T	I	O	N	N	C	C
I	U	P	W	A	R	E	G	F	I	N	A	O
T	R	U	S	T	E	E	D	I	B	I	T	O
E	H	K	O	R	U	M	L	T	Q	N	V	P
D	O	N	A	U	H	P	I	P	U	V	N	E
X	N	Y	R	V	O	L	U	N	T	E	E	R
D	I	R	E	N	C	O	F	G	R	S	P	A
C	H	A	R	I	T	Y	S	H	R	T	U	T
M	A	N	A	G	T	E	G	J	P	O	A	I
W	R	G	D	I	R	E	C	T	O	R	F	V
S	F	J	I	E	M	P	L	R	D	B	C	E

b   Match the words in the puzzle to these definitions.

1   a type of company   *limited*

2   a company equally owned by all the workers

3   a senior manager of a company

4   a person who works without being paid

5   a part of a company, which somebody owns

6   a company which exists mainly not to make money, but to help

7   money that a company makes after taking away costs

8   money that people give to a charity

9   someone who puts money into a company

10   a person who works and receives payment

11   a senior manager of a charity

Language 1

a   Match the halves to make sentences that someone might say after listening to a presentation.

1	Could you just	a	very stimulating talk.
2	One point you raised was that	b	ask what you meant by that?
3	Thank you for a	c	explain the second stage again?
4	I thought your ideas	d	rapid expansion can lead to problems.
5	I'm not sure I quite understood	e	were very interesting.
6	Can I just	f	your point about financial backing.

Communication 1

a Work in pairs. You have just set up a company together. Decide what kind of company it is, and up to five things that the company does.

b Work with a different partner. Ask each other about your companies.

Vocabulary 2

Some words often combine with other words. Match the words 1–6 to their 'partners' a–f.

1	personal	a	sharing
2	flexible	b	leave
3	joint	c	company
4	limited	d	pension
5	profit	e	hours
6	unpaid	f	venture

Language 2

Complete the sentences below with these words.

believe (×2)   aimed   are committed   goal

1 We've always .... to provide quality products at low prices.

2 We .... to preserving the environment.

3 We .... that the customer is always right.

4 Our ultimate .... is to offer a fast, affordable service.

5 We .... in equal opportunities for all employees.

Communication 2

Work in pairs. Discuss how you think these things will change in the future:

• language learning

• your company or college

• workplaces

• companies' attitudes to the environment

Work in groups and discuss your ideas.

Communication activities

 Situation 1

a You are Hanna Charlton's assistant. Look at her business card. Student B will call you to speak to Ms Charlton. Find out who is calling, and why. Explain that Ms Charlton is busy.

Hanna Charlton
Purchasing Manager

Perform Pharmaceuticals

b You are Jenny Wallis's assistant. Look at her business card. Student B will call you to speak to Professor Wallis. Find out who is calling, and why. Put Student B through.

National University

Professor Jenny Wallis
Faculty of Computer Science

Situation 2

You work for the Cabot Hotel. You want companies to send visitors to your hotel and to use it for conferences. Look at the business cards.

a Call George Swanson and try to make an appointment.

 Corporation

George H. Swanson
Sales Director

b Call Nadia Clark and try to make an appointment.

 **SEA Trading Company**

Nadia Clark
General Manager

 Situation 1

You are a manager. Student B is your employee and wants to ask you something. Listen to the request and ask questions to get more details if necessary. Weekly Tuesday morning meetings start next week, but you haven't fixed a time yet. Decide with Student B what the best course of action is.

Situation 2

You are an employee. Student B is your manager. You want to leave early on Friday afternoons. Your mother is unwell and you want to travel to her home every weekend. Leaving early on Friday will make your journey much easier. If necessary, you will work late on Thursdays. Ask for permission.

Look at the information below. Student B will call you. Prepare what you will say.

Situation 1
You are Karl Steiner. Student B has been your supplier for three years and you meet several times a year. You have not been well recently but you are better now. You will have an order for Student B next week. It's a larger order than this time last year.

Situation 2
You are Beatriz Munoz. Student B has been supplying you for one year. You have never met, but you often talk on the phone. You would like to meet Student B to discuss increasing your business. You recently completed a part-time MBA.

Now make two phone calls to Student B using the information below. Prepare what you will say. Remember to make small talk.

Situation 3
You are Claudia Bovinelli. Call Geoff Graham. He is the Purchasing Manager for one of your biggest customers. He has two young children. Call Geoff and ask him when he will place the next order.

Situation 4
You are Marco Panzani. Call Maria Rossi. She is the Sales Director for a company which is a major customer. You meet regularly and you are good friends. She took you out for a very nice dinner last week at a good restaurant. Ask Maria if she needs anything from you.

 Suggest using some of these means of communication, and explain why. Accept or reject Student B's suggestions, and explain why.

Mobile phones: expensive to use; poor quality in noisy locations

Laptops: expensive to buy and use

Video-conferencing: good for meetings for people working at home; cheap software

Two-way radios: cheap to buy and use

 You live an hour from London and work from home. You like using phone and email, but you would like team meetings in London once or twice a month, as you think face-to-face contact is important. You aren't keen on video-conferencing as you have an unreliable telephone line.

Listen to the others' opinions and give yours. Try to agree on a way of working that will be acceptable to all the team.

4 You live and work two hours from Rome. You like email best, with occasional phone calls when necessary. You don't think face-to-face contact is so important and you aren't keen on video-conferencing. You would like a meeting only every three to six months as travelling to meetings takes a long time.

Listen to the others' opinions and give yours. Try to agree on a way of working that will be acceptable to all the team.

4 **Situation 1**

You are a Team Leader for a large design and manufacturing company. Student B is your Project Manager in another country. You both worked on a project that has recently been completed, and Student B has arranged to call you to give feedback. You stayed within budget but you didn't always meet deadlines.

a **Think about what Student B might say about these things, and how you could ask for suggestions.**

- budgets
- deadlines
- problems and solutions
- reviewing performance
- supporting the team
- targets

b **Answer Student B's call and discuss your feedback.**

Situation 2

You are a Product Manager. Student B is a freelance Project Manager in another country. You both worked on a project that has recently been completed, and you have arranged to call Student B to give feedback.

a **Look at your notes. Think about what to say, and think of some suggestions for those areas that need to be improved.**

b **Call Student B and give your feedback.**

Overall - good. The project went quite well.
deadlines ✓
targets ✓
support team ✓
budget ✗
problems/solutions ✗
review performance ✗

5 You are the Managing Director. You think sales have gone down because competitors have been giving special offers. You think a special offer on your leading brand would be a good idea.

Introduce yourself, give your opinions, listen to the others' opinions and then try to agree on the best course of action.

a Read the news article and note the main points.

b Tell Student B about your news story.

c Listen to Student B's news story and ask questions.

China scooter sales lift Piaggio

Italian scooter manufacturer Piaggio says it may have to double output as a result of booming scooter sales in China and India. Piaggio recently signed a deal with Chinese motorcycle maker Zongshen Group to produce 300,000 bikes.

'Piaggio is becoming a little multi-national in its sector,' said Piaggio head Roberto Colaninno. He said, 'The Chinese population which has two- or three-wheeled vehicles is 60 million, which is a low figure with respect to the market potential.'

He said the company also intends to expand in India.

 You are going on a two-day visit to Student B's company, a possible new supplier for you. Call student B and suggest changes. Discuss this schedule for the visit. You are keen to visit two or three different companies during your visit. You would also like to visit an old friend if possible. You will need some space in the schedule for this, but don't tell the supplier why!

Wednesday	
10.30	Arrive. Coffee with senior management
11.30	Tour of factory and offices
1.00	Lunch with Sales and Marketing teams
2.00	Meeting with Marketing Manager
4.00	Meeting with Sales Manager
5.00	Tour of city
7.00	Dinner

Thursday	
9.00	Meeting with Purchasing Manager
10.30	Meeting with Production Manager
11.30	Meeting with Design team
1.00	Lunch with Design and Production teams
2.00	Meeting – negotiations with senior management
4.00	Taxi to station for train home

 Situation 1
Student B is thinking of applying for a job with the company that you work for, and wants to find out about the organizational culture. Tell Student B about your company or imagine you work for the one here.

Situation 2
You are thinking of applying for a job with the company that Student B works for, and you want to find out about the organizational culture. Ask Student B about the company.

John Lewis Partnership

British chain – John Lewis department stores, Waitrose supermarkets.

All employees are 'partners', influence running of company and receive share of profits.

Purpose:
Happiness of partners.

Aims:
Make sufficient profit to stay in business and distribute some profits to partners.

Employ people of ability and integrity who support our principles.

Deal honestly with customers – provide choice, value and service.

Conduct business relationships with integrity and courtesy.

Contribute to local communities.

4 You live and work in the centre of Madrid. You like email, but you prefer phone and video-conferencing. You can get to London quickly and would be happy to have meetings every one or two months.

Listen to the others' opinions and give yours. Try to agree on a way of working that will be acceptable to all the team.

3 a Read the news article and note the main points.

b Listen to Student A's news story and ask questions.

c Tell Student A about your news story.

Coca-Cola's Turkey unit plans to sell shares

Coca-Cola's Turkish unit has announced plans to sell shares in 30% of the company. Coca-Cola Icecek, which has five production plants in Turkey, has not said how much it aims to raise from the issue, which is scheduled for June. It says it has invested $500m in the subsidiary over the last decade and that last year sales reached $556m.

'The Coca-Cola offering has been expected for a long time,' said an analyst at Koc Investment Fusun Bektas. Leading Turkish beer producer Anadolu Efes has a 33% stake in the firm, while the Anadolu Group has a 40% stake.

5 You are the Finance Director. You think sales have gone down because the marketing team have not been promoting the product enough. You think that with more hard work from the marketing people, the product would sell better. You are not keen to spend a lot of extra money on promotion.

Introduce yourself, give your opinions, listen to the others' opinions and then try to agree on the best course of action.

5 You meet Student B at an international conference. Make small talk. Tell Student B about your company, or the one here, and ask Student B about their company.

Adwise advertising agency

Milan

Creative ideas for advertising and special promotions

Plan campaigns

Prepare and produce press, radio and TV ads

Costs for different types of advertising

Help with market research

Situation 1

You work for a shipping company. Student B will call you to place an order. Ask questions to make sure you get all the details you need to complete the form.

Company: ....

Shipping address: ....

....

....

Account no.: ....

Purchase order no.: ....

Order: ....

....

Shipping method: ....

Forwarder: ....

Situation 2

You are a customer. Use the information below to place an order with Student B. Call Student B and give the necessary details.

Company:	JB Stores
Shipping address:	368 Young Street
	Halifax
	Canada
Account no.:	90040072
Purchase order no.:	JBCA10732
Order:	500 x item no. 976283
	100 x item no. 976287
Shipping method:	Sea freight
Forwarder:	CS Containers

Student B, a customer, will call you to ask about two orders.

Situation 1

Ask for the customer's name and purchase order number. The order was dispatched last week. It should arrive today or tomorrow.

Situation 2

Apologize and offer collection and replacement.

Now change roles. You are a customer. Call Student B about two orders.

Situation 3

You ordered 5,000 music CDs but received 4,500.

Situation 4

You ordered a spare part for your computer but the company have sent you the wrong part. You need it urgently.

Look at the information about mobile phone ownership in the UK for 2001 and 2003. Ask Student B questions so you can complete the chart with information for the last six columns for 2003. Answer Student B's questions.

Example

A: *What percentage of people between 15 and 24 years old owned mobile phones in 2003?*

B: *Nearly 90%.*

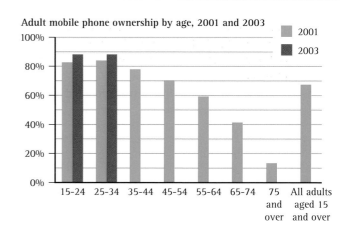

Adult mobile phone ownership by age, 2001 and 2003

2001
2003

15-24 25-34 35-44 45-54 55-64 65-74 75 and over All adults aged 15 and over

5 You are the Marketing Director. You think sales have gone down because advertising has been cut back. You would like to invest in more advertising and start a fresh new ad campaign for the product.

Introduce yourself, give your opinions, listen to the others' opinions and then try to agree on the best course of action.

UNIT 13 PART A PAGE 63

4 a You work in Sales for a large toy company. Prepare a short presentation on recent trends in sales of electronic action games, based on the information in the graph.

Use these notes to help you. Use some, but not all, of the information from the main part.

> *Introduction*
>
> *Your name, company name, type of company, topic of presentation.*
>
> *Main part*
>
> *Many recent developments in technology – possible to make electronic games very cheaply.*
>
> *Parents very keen to buy modern technology; children keen to use it.*
>
> *Children get bored with games quickly, want newer ones.*
>
> *Parents start to feel there is too much modern technology + children should also spend time doing other things.*
>
> *Parents get fed up with buying batteries!*
>
> *Sales figures show fast growth, which has now started to slow down.*
>
> *Summary*
>
> *Need to stay active in this important area.*
>
> *Need to think about developing related – possibly more educational? – games.*

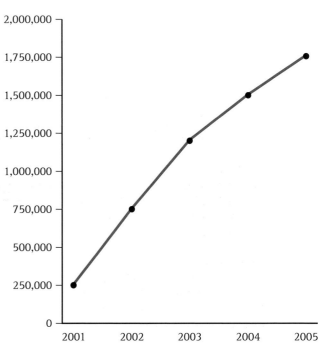

Sales of electronic games in millions 2001–2005

b Give your presentation to Student B. When you have finished, answer student B's questions.

c Listen to Student B's presentation and make notes. When he/she has finished, ask some questions.

Ask Student B ...

... why something happened

... to clarify something

... to explain something again

... to give an example of something

You meet Student A at an international conference. Make small talk. Ask Student A about their company and tell Student A about your company, or the one here.

Northern Power

Manchester

Gas and electricity – 7,000,000 customers

Home and business users

Maintenance of supply infrastructure

Service contracts for business users

24-hour emergency call-out – free to home users

Situation 1
You are thinking of applying for a job with the company that Student A works for, and you want to find out about the organizational culture. Ask Student A about the company.

Situation 2
Student A is thinking of applying for a job with the company that you work for, and wants to find out about the organizational culture. Tell Student A about your company or imagine you work for the one here.

Oxfam

International charity – headquarters in Oxford, volunteers all over the world.

Purpose:
Work with others to overcome poverty and suffering.

Beliefs:
Lives of all human beings are of equal value.
Poverty can be prevented and must be overcome.
Policies and practices can be changed to build a just and safer world.

Aims:
Make a difference.
Innovative and collaborative.
Accountable and cost-effective.

 Situation 1
You work for a medium-sized business which is going to be taken over by a larger multinational company. Listen to Student B, your manager, tell you about probable changes. You have a young family and have recently bought a flat and a new car, so you are concerned about these changes. Ask questions to find out more about them.

Situation 2
You are the manager of a medium-sized business which is going to be taken over by a larger multinational company. Tell Student B, one of your employees, about the probable changes:

- pay increase for some senior staff
- some employees being made redundant
- longer working hours for many employees

Answer Student B's questions.

Help files

Language file 1   Trying to get through

Answering the phone

Hello, [company name].
Good morning. [company name]. Can I help you?
[company name]. Good afternoon.

Asking to speak to someone

I'd like to speak to the Human Resources Director, please.

Can
Could | I speak to the Human Resources Director, please?

Asking the caller's name

Who's calling, please?
Can I ask who's calling, please?
Could I have your name, please?

Saying who you are

This is Jo Benson.
It's David Smith (from [company]).
My name's Tom Wilson.

Asking the caller for more information

Is he/she expecting your call?
Can I ask (you) what it's about?

Connecting the caller

One moment, I'll put you through.
I'm putting you through now.

Saying someone is unavailable

I'm sorry, but he's/she's busy at the moment.
I'm afraid he/she isn't available at the moment.

Offering to take a message

Could
Can | I take a message?

Would you like to leave a message?
Shall I tell him/her you called?

Saying what you will do next

I'll call again (later).
I'll try again (later).
I'll put it in the post.
I'll send an email.

Complete the telephone conversation.

A: Good afternoon. Can I (1) .... you?
B: Could I (2) .... to Miss Danson, please?
A: Can I ask who's (3) ...., please?
B: My (4) .... Cara Walker from TTL.
A: Can I ask (5) .... it's about?
B: I'm (6) .... to discuss our new product range.
A: I'm (7) .... she's busy at the moment. Could I (8) .... a message?
B: No, it's OK, thanks. I'll (9) .... again later, or perhaps I'll (10) .... her an email.
A: All right. Thanks for your call. Goodbye.
B: Goodbye.

Language file 2   Starting and ending a call

Small talk

How are │ you?
        │ things?
        │ the family?

How's │ business?
      │ work?
      │ life?

Did you have a good │ weekend?
                    │ holiday?
                    │ trip?

Not bad, thanks.
Fine, thanks.
Can't complain.
Busy.

And │ you?
    │ yourself?

Giving a reason for calling

I'm calling to ...
I was just calling to ...
I just wanted to ...

Finding out the reason for calling

How can I help you?
What can I do for you?

Ending the conversation politely

Anyway ...
I'll let you get on.
Don't let me keep you.
I won't keep you.
I'm sure you've got plenty to do.
I'd better go (I'm expecting another call).

Put these conversations in the correct order.

1

A:	Hello. James Owen.	[1]
A:	No problem. Bye.	☐
A:	Not bad. What can I do for you?	☐
A:	Hi, Paul. How are you?	☐
A:	Oh, right. Er, it's at 10 o'clock on Monday.	☐
B:	Great, thanks very much. Don't let me keep you. Bye.	☐
B:	Hi, James. It's Paul here.	☐
B:	I'm just calling to check when the next meeting is.	☐
B:	Fine, thanks. And yourself?	☐

2

A:	Bye.	☐
A:	Not bad, can't complain.	☐
A:	Yes, but I'll have to find it. Can I call you back in a minute?	☐
A:	Hello. Claudia Trillo.	[1]
A:	Relaxing. I just stayed at home. What can I do for you?	☐
A:	Hi, Teresa. How are things?	☐
B:	Sure, no problem. Bye for now.	☐
B:	Pretty good, thanks. And you?	☐
B:	Oh, I just wanted to know if you've got Sara's address.	☐
B:	Hi, Claudia. It's Teresa.	☐
B:	How was your weekend?	☐

Language file 1   Making arrangements

Explaining the reason

I'm arranging a meeting to discuss ...
We're organizing a trip in order to find out ...
We're going to have a training session so that we can ...
We'd like to meet up to share ideas about ...

Checking people's availability

Can you give me your availability for [days/dates]?
Could you tell me if you are available on the following dates: [dates]?
Could you let me know when you're free?
Are you free on [days/dates]?

Giving your availability

I'm free on [days/dates].
[day/date] is fine.

I'm (not) available the week of [dates].

I can/can't | make it on / do | [days/dates].

I may/might be able to | make it on / do | [days/dates].

Giving preferences

I'd rather (not) ...
I'd prefer ...
My preferred dates would be ...
The best dates for me are ...

Put the words in these sentences in the correct order.

1 know / available / let / if / Could / you / Monday / are / on / me / you ?
2 me / Tuesday / day / for / be / best / would / The
3 a / discuss / to / have / project / We're / meeting / to / going / the
4 I'm / I'm / of / not / the / week / afraid / 23rd / available / the
5 week / availability / Can / for / give / next / you / me / your ?
6 make / morning / it / on / can't / I / Friday.
7 when / you're / Could / free / know / me / you / let ?
8 able / Thursday / may / to / do / I / be

Language file 2   Emails

Subject line

Keep this as short and clear as possible. Choose key words that will explain quickly what your email is about.

When you reply, you should normally keep the same subject line. But if most of your reply is about something different, you can change the subject line.

If you use the 'Reply' button for the email you've received, the same subject line, with 'Re:' in front of it, will be entered automatically.

Greeting

Informal	Hi Paul
↑	Hello Paul
	Paul
	Dear Paul
	Dear Paul Jones
↓	
Formal	Dear Mr Jones

Opening comment

I hope you're well.
I hope you had a good holiday.
I hope you had a good weekend.

Introduction

A short, clear sentence that explains what you are writing about:

I am writing to | ask ...
| check ...
| explain ...
| clarify ...
| confirm ...
| complain ...
| apologize ...

I'd like to ...
I just wanted to ...

As you know, ...
You may remember ...

Main point

Keep your message short and simple. People don't like reading long emails, so keep to the subject.
DON'T WRITE EVERYTHING IN CAPITALS, BECAUSE THIS IS LIKE SHOUTING AND MAKES PEOPLE THINK YOU ARE ANGRY!

Concluding sentences

I hope this is | useful.
 | helpful.

Do let me know if | anything isn't clear.
 | you need any more information.
 | you can't read the attachment.

Can you let me know by Tuesday?
Can you let me know if you can't make it?
Can you call me about this tomorrow?

Attachments

Please find attached ...
I have attached ...
Attached is ...
Do let me know if you can't read the attachment.

Signing off

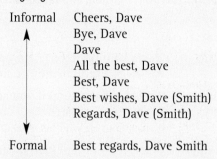

Informal   Cheers, Dave
 Bye, Dave
 Dave
 All the best, Dave
 Best, Dave
 Best wishes, Dave (Smith)
 Regards, Dave (Smith)

Formal   Best regards, Dave Smith

Signature

This should contain information about your position in the company and other ways of contacting you, for example, your direct phone number, mobile number or fax number. You can usually add this automatically to every email.

Match the sentence halves from A and B to make a complete email.

	A			B
1	Dear		a	you're well.
2	I hope		b	attached her reports.
3	I am just writing to		c	remember she helped us a lot last year.
4	It will be on		d	best, Lisa
5	As you know,		e	Monday 23rd at 10 a.m.
6	You may		f	confirm the details of our meeting.
7	I have		g	seeing you there.
8	Do let me know		h	Susan
9	Looking forward to		i	the Marketing Director will be there.
10	All the		j	if you can't read the attachments.

Formal		Informal
Inviting	Would you like to have dinner? We would like to invite you to ...	(How) do you fancy going out to dinner? Do you want to go out for dinner?
Asking for a reply	We would be grateful if you could confirm whether you can attend. Please confirm whether you are able to join us.	Let me know if you can come. Give me a call if you can make it.
Thanking	Thank you for your kind invitation. I am very grateful for your invitation.	Thanks for the invite. Thanks for your invitation.
Accepting	I can confirm that I will be able to attend. I would very much like to come. I would be delighted to attend.	Yes, I'd love to come. Yes, I'd love to. Yes, I'd really like that.
Rejecting	I regret I am unable to attend due to a prior engagement. I would like to accept, but ...	I'm afraid I can't make it as I've already made plans. Sorry, I've got something else on then.
Stalling	I may have another commitment at that time. I will confirm by the end of the week.	I might not be able to. I'll let you know by Friday. I'll have to check and get back to you.

a   Read these two emails – a formal invitation and a reply. Tick (✓) the lines which are formal enough, and change the lines which are too informal.

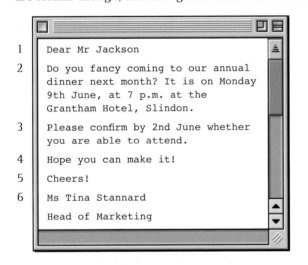

1   Dear Mr Jackson

2   Do you fancy coming to our annual dinner next month? It is on Monday 9th June, at 7 p.m. at the Grantham Hotel, Slindon.

3   Please confirm by 2nd June whether you are able to attend.

4   Hope you can make it!

5   Cheers!

6   Ms Tina Stannard

Head of Marketing

7   Hi Tina

8   Thank you for your kind invitation to the annual dinner.

9   I'm afraid I can't make it as I'm playing football then.

10 I hope the evening goes well and look forward to working with you again.

11 Best wishes

12 Pete

b   Read these two emails – an informal invitation and a reply. Tick (✓) the lines which are informal enough, and change the lines which are too formal.

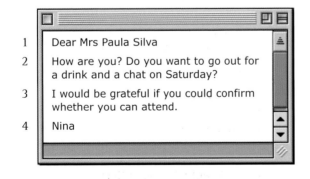

1   Dear Mrs Paula Silva

2   How are you? Do you want to go out for a drink and a chat on Saturday?

3   I would be grateful if you could confirm whether you can attend.

4   Nina

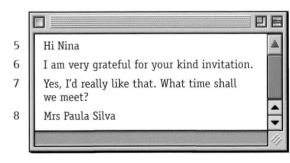

5   Hi Nina

6   I am very grateful for your kind invitation.

7   Yes, I'd really like that. What time shall we meet?

8   Mrs Paula Silva

Language file 1   Suggestions

Asking for suggestions

Does anyone have any suggestions/ideas?
What can we do about this? Any ideas?
Is there anything we can do to resolve this problem?

Making suggestions

I wonder if we could ...
I wonder whether we could ...

What about contacting them directly?
Have you considered installing a new system?

Could we ask the staff for their input?
Why don't we do some market research?

We could see what people think.
(I think) we need to make some changes.
I think we should ...

Let's try this for a month.

Accepting suggestions

That sounds like a good | solution.
                     | idea.

That could work.
That's a good idea.
That's worth a try.

Rejecting suggestions

I've thought about it, but ...
That's a good idea, but ...
It might work, but ...

Fill in the gaps with one word to complete the sentences.

1 Does .... have any suggestions?
2 Have you .... a new phone system?
3 That .... like a good idea.
4 I .... whether we could ask the customers.
5 That's a .... idea, but it could be expensive.
6 Why .... we write some instructions?
7 Yes, that's .... a try.

Language file 2   Opinions

Asking for opinions

What do you think?
Don't you think that ...?
Do you agree?

Giving your opinion

I think they should use the phone more.
If you ask me, they write too many emails.
I don't think a monthly meeting is necessary.

Agreeing completely

I agree.
Good point (I didn't think of that).
I couldn't agree more.
Good idea.

Agreeing but not completely

I see what you mean,
I suppose so, |
That's true,   but ...
That's a good point,
Yes,
Hmm ... I'm not sure about that.

Match the sentence beginnings 1–7 to the endings a–g.

1 I couldn't
2 That's a good point,
3 What do
4 I see what you
5 If you ask
6 I suppose so, but
7 Good point. I

a me, that's too expensive.
b you think?
c agree more!
d didn't think of that.
e mean, but staff won't like it.
f but it will take a long time.
g I'm not keen on the idea.

to make a phone call
to phone someone
to call someone
to call someone on a mobile

to send something by email
to send an email (to someone)
to email (something to) someone

to receive | an email / an attachment | (from someone)

to send something by fax
to send a fax (to someone)
to fax (something to) someone
to receive a fax (from someone)

a video conference
video-conferencing

Choose the correct words in these sentences.

1 We *sent to all our customers / sent all our customers* an email.
2 We don't often send *documents by fax / documents through fax* now.
3 Has she *emailed the report Martin / emailed the report to Martin* yet?
4 I *phone called / called* Steffi and left a message.
5 I received a fax *by Anna / from Anna* the other day.
6 I received *from your manager an email / an email from your manager* last week.
7 I'll have to call Neil *on his mobile / to his mobile*.
8 Could you *phone Jim / phone to Jim* and check the figures?

UNIT 4

Language file 1   Writing a covering letter

Saying why you are writing

I would like / I am writing | to apply for the | post / position | of ... advertised in | this week's [newspaper/magazine]. / [newspaper/magazine] on [date].

Writing about experience

You | will / can | see from my enclosed CV that ...

I have worked for Z-Plan | for three years. / since 2003. (from the past to the present)

I have worked for | two / several / a number of | major banks. (at some time in the past)

I worked for GTC | for three years. / from 2001 to 2004. (at a specific time in the past) / in 2003.

Writing about skills

I have good | communication / computer / time-management / technical | skills.

I am creative / dynamic / energetic / self-motivated / literate / numerate / hard-working / flexible / patient.

Writing about interests, plans

I am interested in | fashion. (noun) / working with visitors. (-*ing* form)

I am keen on / I enjoy | sport. (noun) / swimming. (-*ing* form) | (= I like doing this)

I am keen to | pursue a career in this area. / improve my IT skills. | (= I want to do this)

Writing about qualifications

I have | a degree in ... / a diploma in ... / school certificates in ... / good qualifications. / a clean driving licence.

Closing

I am available for interview	the week of August 11th.
	at any time.
	at your convenience.

If you require any further information, please do not hesitate to contact me.

I look forward to hearing from you.

Yours sincerely, (when beginning *Dear* + name)
Yours faithfully, (when beginning *Dear Sir/Mdam*)

Match the information a–k to the different parts 1–11 of the covering letter.

a Closing statement.

b Give details of qualifications, skills, interests, etc. Keep it concise.

c The name (and position if you know it) of the person you are writing to, and the company name and address.

d Reason for writing: Say clearly and simply why you are writing, without any details. Avoid using contractions (e.g. *I'd like*) in a formal letter.

e Refer to any enclosures and offer to provide more details if necessary. You could also say if there are any dates when you are not available.

f The date. (Don't include the day.)

g Write your name under your signature, as your signature may not be easy to read. If you are writing from a company, you should write your position in the company under your name, as in an email. If you are enclosing another document, such as your CV, write *enc.* after your name.

h Greeting: *Dear* followed by:
Mr + surname for a man
Ms + surname for a woman
Mrs + surname for a married woman (but use *Ms* unless you know that the woman you're writing to uses *Mrs*).

i Your address and contact details, but not your name. In a personal letter, these should be in the top right-hand corner. In a business letter, you will probably use headed paper, which has the company's details printed on it.

j 'Farewell'. *Yours sincerely* or *Yours faithfully* are appropriate in a formal letter.

k Give some details of your experience, and refer to your CV.

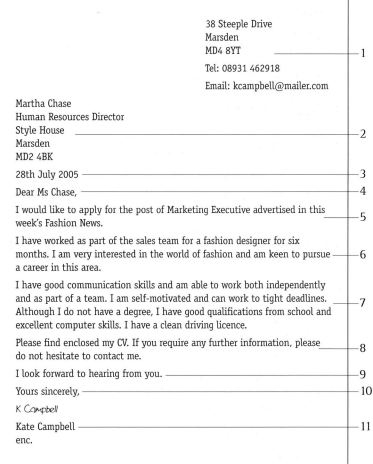

38 Steeple Drive
Marsden
MD4 8YT —————— 1

Tel: 08931 462918

Email: kcampbell@mailer.com

Martha Chase
Human Resources Director
Style House ————————— 2
Marsden
MD2 4BK

28th July 2005 ————————— 3

Dear Ms Chase, ———————— 4

I would like to apply for the post of Marketing Executive advertised in this week's Fashion News. ————— 5

I have worked as part of the sales team for a fashion designer for six months. I am very interested in the world of fashion and am keen to pursue —— 6 a career in this area.

I have good communication skills and am able to work both independently and as part of a team. I am self-motivated and can work to tight deadlines. —— 7 Although I do not have a degree, I have good qualifications from school and excellent computer skills. I have a clean driving licence.

Please find enclosed my CV. If you require any further information, please —— 8 do not hesitate to contact me.

I look forward to hearing from you. ————————— 9

Yours sincerely, ————————— 10

K Campbell

Kate Campbell ————————— 11
enc.

Talking about your good points

What can you offer this company?
What have you got to offer us?
Why should we employ you?
Why do you think we should employ you?

I'm creative and dynamic – my track record in my current job proves that.
My track record shows that I have good experience.
As you can see from my CV, I have a strong background in ...
I'm self-motivated and good at organizing my time.
I think I'm flexible in the way I plan my work.
I'm keen to learn.

Talking about negative points

What about negative points?
What do you think your negative points are?
What areas do you think you could improve in?
What might your current employer want you to improve?

One fault is that I'm a bit of a perfectionist.
I sometimes try too hard to get everything exactly right.
Some people might say I talk too much.

Recently I've tried to ...
I'm working on this at the moment.
I think I've improved a lot in this area.

Talking about future plans

What about the future?
Do you know where you want to be in two years' time?

Where do you see yourself | in five years?
| five years from now?

Do you plan to study for further qualifications?

I would like to be the manager of a whole division in five years.
I hope to climb the career ladder as fast as I can.

Talking about experience

Have you ever done ... before?

Yes, I have. I've done that a lot in my current job.
Yes, I have. I did it in my previous job.

No, I haven't, but I'm willing to learn if it's necessary for this job.

Answering 'difficult' questions

Your exam results are not as good as they could be, are they?
That's true, but I believe my practical experience since then shows what I can do.

I see that you didn't complete your Diploma course. Why was that?
I decided that the theoretical aspects weren't for me, and I wanted to gain a practical working knowledge of the industry.

Why are you leaving your current job?
I'm very happy in my current job, but I feel your company would offer more opportunities to develop my career.

Some people might say you're very young to take on such a position.
I would say that age is not the most important thing in management.

What would you say to that?
I can understand that comment, but ...

Asking questions

I know you have a programme ... What would that involve exactly?
I understand that you have a system ... Could you explain it in more detail?
I believe that you are planning ... How is that going to operate?

Choose the best answer for each interview question.

1 What can you offer this company?
   a I'm a kind, friendly person.
   b I'm self-motivated, and I have good experience in this industry.
   c I get up very early every morning and work very hard.

2 Why do you think we should employ you?
   a I think selling things is interesting and I would like to learn more about it.
   b I need to get experience in sales before I start work in my father's company.
   c I'm creative and dynamic, and I have an excellent track record in sales.

3 What areas do you think you could improve in?
   a My IT skills are not up-to-date, but I'm doing an IT course at the moment.
   b None. I think I have all the necessary skills to do this job.
   c I haven't got very good communication skills. They could be much better.

4 Why are you leaving your current job?
   a My current job is OK, but I need to earn more money and work fewer hours.
   b I like my current job, but I want to develop my management skills more.
   c I don't like my current job at all. It's really hard work, and I don't like the company.

5 I see that you don't have a university degree. Why is that?
   a I don't think university courses help you very much in the workplace.
   b I decided to train in the practical aspects of the industry. I'm not very academic.
   c I think university is boring, and you don't earn any money when you're a student.

6 Where do you see yourself in five years?
   a I'd like to be in a better job in five years, but I don't want to be a manager.
   b I don't really know. That's a very difficult question to answer, isn't it?
   c I'm very ambitious. I hope to be in senior management in five years.

7 Have you ever worked abroad before?
   a No, I haven't, but I have travelled and I'm sure I would enjoy the challenge.
   b No, I haven't.
   c No, I haven't, and I don't want to because I don't speak any foreign languages.

8 Do you have any questions?
   a I believe the trains aren't very good here. What time does the next one leave?
   b I understand you have a staff training programme. Could you tell me more about it?
   c I know you don't pay very well, but what's the salary for this job?

Language file 1   Permission

Asking for permission

For more 'difficult' requests, we usually use less direct language:

More direct (easier requests)	Can I go to lunch at 12.15 today? Could I come in a bit late tomorrow?
↕	Is it OK if I go (home) early this afternoon? Do you mind if I work at home tomorrow?
Less direct (more difficult requests)	I was wondering if I could have a day off. Would it be all right if I finished the accounts next week?

Giving permission

Sure.
Fine.
No problem.
(That's) OK.

When we give permission, we often add a condition:

Permission	Condition
(Well,) I suppose so,	but you'll have to do extra next week.
(Well,) OK,	but make it a quick call, please.

Refusing permission

Try to avoid saying 'No'. Use less direct language, and give a reason:

I'm afraid that's not possible. We're going to be very busy that day.
Sorry, but I'm on holiday then, so you need to be here.
I'm sorry. The problem is that our meetings always start at 9.00.
Is there another way round it?

When we refuse permission, we often suggest an alternative:

I'm afraid you can't ... but what about ...?
I don't think that's possible, but maybe you could ... instead.

Put the words in these conversations in the correct order.

1 A: on / I / Could / early / Friday / finish ?
   B: possible / be / I'm / not / going / afraid / to / that's
2 A: OK / go / now / if / lunch / it / I / Is / to ?
   B: have / come / so / to / early / I / you'll / but / suppose / back
3 A: I / tomorrow / the / went / it / if / be / to / dentist / OK / morning / Would ?
   B: sorry / I'm. / not / here / I'm / be / going / to
4 A: I / a / if / call / you / make / mind / Do / personal ?
   B: long / but / take / Well / don't / OK / too
5 A: my / dates / wondering / could / was / if / change / I / I / the / for / holiday
   B: another / but / when / could / Sorry / go / isn't / there / week / you

Language file 2 — Delegating

Introducing the request

| Could you | do something for me? |
| Can I ask you to | do some research ...? |

Asking what the task is

What (exactly) is it?
What kind of ... is it?

Making the request

Would you check ...?
Do you think you could check ...?
I don't suppose you could check ...

| I wonder | |
| I was wondering | if you could ... |

Asking for more details

What day do you want to have the meeting?
How soon do we need to do it?
How soon do you need it?
How urgent is it?

Giving details, including deadlines

Can you report back in a month?
Can you get back to me when you've set it up?

Agreeing to do the task

Yes, I think I could ...
No problem.
Fine.
Sure.
OK.
Is it OK if I do it by ...?

Correct the mistakes.

1 Could you to do something for me?
2 What exactly is?
3 Can I ask that you do something?
4 I don't suppose could you do a progress report.
5 Can you sending me the files next week?
6 Yes, I'm thinking I could do that.

Vocabulary file — Verb combinations

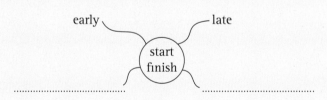

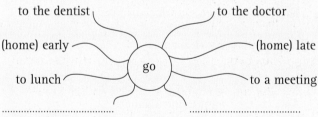

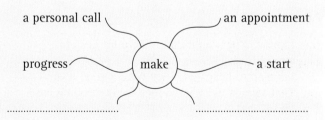

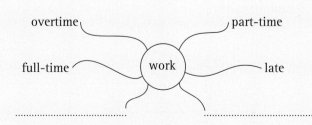

Choose the correct words in these sentences. One or two words may be correct.

1 Steve usually *makes / takes / has* a break at about 10.30.
2 We're not allowed to *make / bring / have* personal calls at work.
3 I'm going to *work / finish / start* late today, to finish this report.
4 Shall we *take / go / have* to lunch now?
5 Kim isn't well, so she's *having / making / taking* a day off.
6 Susana had to *take / bring / go* her son to work last week, because the school was closed.
7 I need to *take / have / bring* some time off tomorrow.
8 I have to *go / make / take* to the dentist.

Language file 1 Giving and receiving feedback

Thanking

Everyone	
We	would like to thank you very much for all your hard work.
I	

I/We would like to say how much we appreciate all your efforts.
I/We really appreciate everything you've done.
I/We are very grateful for all your work.

Responding to thanks

You're welcome. It was a pleasure.
It was a very enjoyable project to work on.

Praising

| We were | |
| I was | pleased that you … |

| We're | |
| I'm | very pleased with what you did. |

It was good that you …

Your … was very effective.

Responding to praise

Good.
Thank you.
Excellent. I'm glad to hear that.

Criticizing

There are always areas which can be improved …

Spending control	could
	have been better.
	should

Note: *Should* is stronger than *could*.

You need to improve team communication.
And another point to think about: …

Asking for advice

Have you got any	suggestions
	for dealing with that?
	ideas

How could I improve that?
What could I do about that?

Giving advice

You	could
	have more frequent budget reviews.
	should

| Why don't you | |
| Why not | send out weekly updates? |

Have you	thought of
	sending out weekly updates?
	considered

| How about | |
| What about | working more closely with …? |

Responding to advice

That's a good idea. Thanks for that.
That sounds good. I'll try that next time.

Match the sentences 1–5 to the responses a–e.

1 How about making each team responsible for their own budget?
2 Quality control could have been better.
3 The team thought your communication was very effective.
4 We're very grateful for everything you've done.
5 You need to meet your deadlines.

a I know. What could I do to help me keep to the schedule?
b I'm glad to hear that. They were a good team.
c That sounds like a good idea for controlling costs. I'll try that.
d Yes, there were problems with quality. How could I improve that?
e You're welcome. It was a pleasure.

Language file 2   Responding to feedback

Accepting criticism

Yes, that's true.
Yes, I realize that.
That's a fair point.
I agree.

Apologizing

I'm (really) sorry (about that).
I can only apologize.

Offering a solution

I'll make sure this doesn't happen again.
I'll pass this feedback on to the rest of the team.
In future, I'll ...

Asking for more details

I'm not exactly sure what you mean.
I don't think I get what you mean.
I'm not sure I understand.

Could you explain that | a bit more?
                      | in more detail?
Can you give me specific examples?
Can I just check what you mean?
Can we clarify that?

Rejecting criticism

I'm not sure that's entirely fair.
I'm afraid I can't accept that.
I don't (entirely) agree with you on that.

Giving reasons

I did my best but | we didn't always receive the information.
                  | we were let down by ...

I did everything I could with the resources available.
It was a difficult project for a number of reasons ...

Write complete sentences using these prompts.

1 I / sure / happen again.
2 I / best but / always receive / information.
3 I / apologize.
4 / afraid / accept /
5 / future, / control / finances / carefully.
6 Can / give / examples?
7 I / sure / fair.
8 / fair point.
9 / did / could / resources /
10 I / think / what / mean.

Vocabulary file   Performance

set
meet | a deadline
miss

achieve | a target
set | targets

stay within (the) |
go over | budget

train
support | the team
motivate

deal with | problems
           | questions

come up with | solutions
             | answers

keep people | informed
            | motivated
            | happy

review | performance
       | progress

recommend | changes
          | improvements

Complete the text with the correct form of expressions on the left.

Generally, the project went very well indeed. You
(1) ...., so everyone knew exactly what
they had to do, and largely because of that nobody
(2) .... – everything was done on time.
There were some problems, but you (3) ....
them quickly by (4) .... that worked well.
Unfortunately the project (5) ....
so you will have to control spending better next time, and make
sure that everyone (6) ...., as costs are an
important issue in the company at the moment. I think you need
to (7) .... more with practical help and
ideas, and (8) .... better – sometimes
people didn't know what was happening. You could
(9) .... with each team member more
regularly, so that they know how they are doing, and you can
(10) .... to help them do their job better.

Language file 1 · Talking about business news

Did you hear about those two guys who started Google?
Have you seen the article about NPL?
Have you heard the latest about bubble.com ?
Hey, this is interesting.

No, what about it/them?
What's that?

It says they've made a loss this year.
I've heard that they're going to merge.
They've both become billionaires now.
easyJet's passenger numbers have gone up.

That doesn't surprise me, actually.
Really? Where did you hear that?

| It was on the | front | page of ... |
| | back | |

I saw a headline in ...
There's an article about it in ...
It was on a TV news bulletin last night.

There was a quote	
There was a quote by him	in all the national newspapers.
He was quoted	

Put these sentences in the correct order to make two separate conversations.

a No, what does it say?
b I've heard that he's going to be the new CEO of Energon.
c No, what about him?
d Have you seen the article about Digitalis?
e That doesn't surprise me – they've got the technology.
f Really? Where did you hear that?
g Did you hear about Malcolm Nettles?
h It says they're expanding into mobile phones.

Language file 2

Talking about websites

You can find out about ...
You have to type your postcode.
You can choose ...
If you want, you can add your date of birth.

You can search for ...
There's a facility to search for ...
You can search by ...

You can click on the map.
There's a clickable map.
There are links to the regions.
You can browse the regions.
You can browse by region.

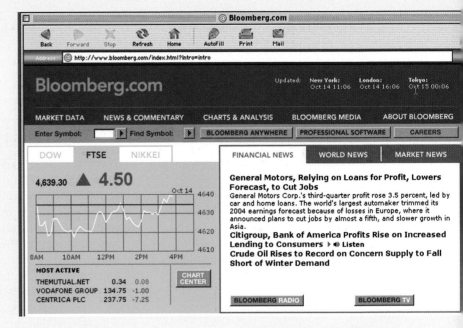

Match these descriptions to parts of the Bloomberg web page.

1 There are links to other forms of news from Bloomberg.
2 If you want, you can quickly view the latest prices from three stock markets.
3 There's a link to more information on the Bloomberg company.
4 You can choose from three different categories of news.
5 There's a facility to download computer programs for your business.
6 You can click on a button for more charts.

Vocabulary file   Websites

browse   home page   search   scroll

menus

drop-down
menu

links

Complete these sentences with words from above.

1 It's helpful to include .... to other related websites.
2 Very long web pages aren't a good idea because people have to ....
   up and down a lot to find what they want.
3 .... should be fairly short, so that users don't have to spend a long
   time making their choice.
4 Users who know exactly what they want can use the .... facility to
   find it quickly.
5 It's important to have a clear, attractive ...., as it gives a good first
   impression.
6 Users who are not sure exactly what they are looking for usually prefer to
   .... the site.
7 .... are good for long but 'limited' lists such as countries and dates.

Language file 1   Writing minutes

Minutes should be easy to read, so that people can quickly find the information they need. Instead of long sentences, use headings, bullet points and lists.

Action points should say:
- **who** is doing something
- **what** they are doing
- **when** they are doing it

heading —— **5. Product updates**

Funcam single use camera, Executive camera and Mini-digital camera

bullet points ——— • Sales figures

action points ——— • Forecasts for following year

Action:

who ——— David Miles (Marketing) – Continue to do

what ——— market research on these products by

when ——— 20th September.

Sonia Collins (Sales)   Keep staff posted with monthly sales figures.

Rewrite these minutes so that they are easier to read.

> We had a very interesting meeting, and decided that next year we should focus our attention on our four key markets, which are France, Spain, Italy and Poland. We think it would be a good idea to set up a strategy team to do this. Pete Young, who is the Director of the Planning Department, is going to decide how many people should be in the strategy team, and who those people should be. He says he is going to do this by 30th May. We also think that we should focus on our bestselling products, which are books, CDs and videos. The Director of the Sales Department says she is going to provide sales figures for these products in those four markets. She is going to do this by 16th May. Her name is Pauline Walker.

Language file 2   Taking part in meetings

(See Unit 3 for suggestions and opinions.)

Asking for clarification

Sorry, I didn't (quite) catch that. What did you say?
Sorry, I missed that last point.

Can you expand on that?

I'm not sure I understand how that would help.
Sorry, I don't understand what you're getting at.
Sorry, I don't (quite) follow you.
Sorry, I'm not (quite) with you.
I'm afraid I don't follow what you're saying.
What exactly do you mean by ...?

Reviewing what people have said

Shall we (just) go over what we've said so far?
I'd (just) like to recap what's been said.
Let me (just) go over that.
Can we (just) go over what you're saying?
You're saying that by focusing on costs, we can increase profits.
You think we would get more sales by reducing prices.
So, you mean ...

Deciding who is going to do things

So, first of all, we need to decide ...
Second, somebody needs to think about ...
We need to think about dates for all of this.

Put the words in these sentences in the correct order.

1 expand / that / you / on / Can ?
2 recap / what's / like / said / I'd / to / been
3 costs / think / needs / Somebody / to / about
4 at / don't / getting / I / Sorry, / what / understand / you're
5 over / Let / that / just / me / go
6 schedule / We / about / to / this / think / a / need / for
7 I / saying / follow / afraid / what / I'm / you're / don't
8 go / you're / what / we / saying / over / just / Can ?

Vocabulary file   The agenda

Complete the sentences below with these words.

item	next meeting	agenda	matters arising
participants	apologies	minutes	any other business (AOB)

1 Sorry, I didn't have time to do a list of ...., but I think we all know each other anyway, don't we?
2 So, is everyone happy with the .... of the last meeting?
3 Right, we need to think about a date for the ....
4 OK, time's running out. I think we should move on to the next .... now.
5 Now, ... from the last meeting. Have we met all the deadlines we agreed then?
6 Mark sends his .... He's dealing with an urgent problem in the factory.
7 Does anyone have .... to discuss?
8 Did everyone get an ....? Good. So we all know what we're going to discuss.

UNIT 9

Language file 1   Plans

Talking about plans

The goal The aim Our target	is to maintain sales of our services to ...

I plan to I'm going to I aim to I hope to	visit all the companies.

Explaining plans

That way I should have time to go back ...
That means you can start calling your biggest customers.

If she makes the list, it will be much quicker.

If I call them all next week, I can start visiting the following week.
If you start sooner, you could make more appointments.
If we don't keep the database up-to-date, we might lose track.
If you divide up your area, you should be more effective.

Choose the correct words in these sentences.

1 That *means / mean* we can keep the project on track.
2 If we start now, we should *to finish / finish* it today.
3 The goal is *to / for* find new markets.
4 If you *not plan / don't plan* carefully, you could miss the deadline.
5 I plan to *call / calling* everyone back tomorrow.
6 If I work late this week, I might *make up / making up* the lost time.
7 We *aiming / aim* to complete the report next week.
8 Our targets *is / are* to reduce costs and increase sales.

Language file 2   Changing schedules

Requesting changes

Could we put the last meeting off till my next visit?
Do you think we could cut down the tour?

I wonder if we could do that in the afternoon.
I was wondering if we could make some small changes.

Is it at all possible to finish slightly earlier?
Would it be possible to put lunch back an hour?

Is there any chance of putting off one of the meetings until Wednesday?
Is there any chance that we could start a bit later?

I don't suppose we could have a shorter lunch break, could we?

Agreeing to changes

That should be possible.
That shouldn't be a problem.
No problem.

Yes, we can certainly cut down the tour.
Yes, I think we can.

I'm sure that will be | all right.
                   | fine.

Suggesting new times

Shall we say, 3.30 to 5, meeting with MD?
Let's say 12 o'clock.
How about lunch at 12.30?

Refusing changes

That could be difficult.
That might be a problem.
It may not be easy to change that.
It won't be possible to ... because ... . But we can probably ...

Make these conversations more polite, using expressions that include the words in brackets.

Example

  A: Make the meeting shorter.   (think, could)
  B: Yes.   (should, possible)

  A: *Do you think we could make the meeting shorter?*
  B: *That should be possible.*

1 A: I want to have dinner earlier.   (wonder, could)
   B: No.   (easy, change)
2 A: Meet me at the airport   (wondering, could)
   B: Sure.   (fine)
3 A: I want a tour of the factory. (would, possible)
   B: Yes.   (shouldn't, problem)
4 A: Change the meeting to Thursday. (chance, of)
   B: No.   (might, difficult)
5 A: I want a sightseeing tour. (suppose, could)
   B: Yes.   (sure, fine)

Vocabulary file 1   Verb combinations

keep	track (of ...) up-to-date an appointment a list on time on track
keep something	up-to-date on track

lose	track a list time

make	a suggestion an appointment a list time

make up | time

meet | a deadline

miss	an appointment a deadline

put in	extra time more hours

run	behind/late behind schedule on time

set | a deadline

Put the lines in the correct order to complete the text. Number 1 is in the correct place.

1 Nowadays, our schedules are tight and it's important to keep a
2 time from beginning to end, but if there is a problem and you miss a
3 deadlines. We advise employees on time management. For example, make
4 up-to-date, so that if anyone needs to check the schedule, we don't lose
5 project on track. So, dates are agreed at the start and everyone has to meet their
6 behind for a long time, so the sooner we know, the better.
7 track of anything. Like all companies, we prefer our projects to run on
8 the lost time. These problems usually get bigger if we let the project run
9 deadline, tell others quickly so that they can look for ways of making up
10 lists of tasks, but prioritize – put them in order of importance. Keep records

Vocabulary file 2 — Phrasal verbs

Phrasal verbs with no object

I was off sick yesterday so I need to **catch up** today.   (get up-to-date)
This new idea will never **catch on**!   (become popular)

Sorry, I'm going to be late. Something has **come up**.   (happen unexpectedly)
If the plan **comes off**, we could make a lot of money.   (succeed)

I'm afraid I've got to **head off** soon.   (leave)
What time do you need to **head back** to the office?   (return)

Phrasal verbs with an object

All of the phrasal verbs below can be separated by the object:

We need to **cut down** the schedule.
We need to **cut** the schedule **down**.   (reduce)

If the object of one of these phrasal verbs is a pronoun, it must go between the verb and the preposition/particle:

We need to **cut** it **down**.

The pronoun cannot go at the end:
~~We need to cut down it.~~

It won't be possible to **cut out** those stages.
It won't be possible to **cut** those stages **out**.   (remove)
It won't be possible to **cut** them **out**.

Late deliveries have **held up** the project.
Late deliveries have **held** the project **up**.   (delay)
Late deliveries have **held** it **up**.

Let's **put off/back** your presentation to the next day.
Let's **put** your presentation **off/back** to the next day.   (change to a later date/time)
Let's **put** it **off/back** to the next day.

Complete the sentences with phrasal verbs from above in the correct form.

1 Please start without me. I don't want to .... you ....
2 I'm running so far behind, I don't think I'll ever ....
3 We need to .... this project or it will take too long to complete.
4 We're running out of time. Shall we .... our final decision to next week?
5 My secretary will call me if anything .... while I'm away.
6 Why don't we .... these two parts? They aren't really necessary.

Language file 1   Advertising

Comparatives and superlatives

There's never been a better time to buy one of these.
Recording your favourite programmes is easier than ever.
The ZXM is quieter than anything we have produced before.
This model is more sophisticated than any others currently available.

APC – the sleekest palmtop you are ever likely to use.
The longest bed in its class.
The Academy Hotel – for the most comfortable rooms in town.
We provide the most economical service you will find.

Complete these sentences with the correct comparative or superlative form of the adjective in brackets.

1 This machine is simply .... (good) model on the market right now.
2 We don't know of a .... (advanced) system anywhere!
3 Mekanik Ltd guarantee that this is .... (affordable) office furniture that you can find.
4 Tests have proved that the 3-door Cresta is .... (economical) the Fina.
5 We are .... (busy) bus company in the city, and our service is .... (friendly) any of the others!
6 Even though this is .... (sophisticated) alarm system in Europe, it is .... (easy) to use, and it's not .... (expensive).
7 You won't find the same model .... (cheap) anywhere today.
8 Readers of *Business* magazine voted our hotel .... (comfortable) in the UK last year.

Conditionals

Get £50 off if you apply now.
If you don't go, you'll never know what it's like!
If you test drive the new Tamara, you won't be disappointed.
You might be pleasantly surprised if you've never used a G-Tech before.

Write complete sentences using these prompts.

1 If / buy / our latest PC / we / include / free software package.
2 / you / not believe us / test / new 'GameMan' at one of our stores.
3 / could regret it / if / not book today.
4 If / your photographs / look like this / be delighted with the 'AutoFocus'.
5 If / not / completely satisfied / we / give / full refund.
6 Buy this / if / want / stay ahead!

Language file 2   Talking about brands

Multiform software is | known / well known / famous | for its flexibility.

Multiform has a | reputation / name | for being a complete all-in-one design package.

This reputation was achieved without expensive advertising.

Multiform got its reputation mainly | by / through | word of mouth.

It's | commonly used by / well known to | professional designers.

Match the sentence halves.

1 Bridgestone tyres are well known to
2 Dell Computers have a name for
3 DMZ has a reputation for
4 Lasertech are well
5 Pokemon toys
6 Spain is famous

a got their reputation by word of mouth.
b known for the quality of their products.
c for its good wines.
d motor racing drivers.
e lasting a long time.
f manufacturing low-priced clothes.

Vocabulary file   Adjectives

advanced	using very new technology
affordable	not too expensive
comfortable	nice to sit on, live in, etc.
compatible	can be used with different equipment
comprehensive	complete, having everything you need
easy-to-use	not difficult to use
economical	not expensive to use
flexible	can be used in different situations
portable	easy to carry and move around
sleek and stylish	looks smooth and shiny, and has a very attractive design
sophisticated	complex and made with great skill

Complete these adverts with adjectives from above.

1 At only €499, this is the most .... computer ever!
2 If you're concerned about how much fuel you use, you will be very happy with the new Limba – it's the most .... car in its class.
3 The Photo Magic software package is .... with all PC operating systems.
4 We guarantee that these chairs are so .... your office staff will never complain about back pains again!
5 If you're fashion-conscious, you can't go wrong with our latest mobile phone – it's ....
6 We provide the most .... delivery package you will find – we will do everything that you need, from beginning to end.
7 At last, a genuinely .... laptop – at only 3.5kg, you really can take it anywhere.
8 Our watches are highly ...., designed for busy, adventurous people who demand many different uses in a watch.

Language file 1 — Taking and placing orders

Can I just take some details from you so that we can track the order?

Can I check which shipping forwarder you want us to use?

Could I have your company name and account number?

I'd like to check some details with you if that's OK.

I | don't suppose / wonder if | you could spell that for me.

Can you give me your (own) purchase order number?

Could you tell me what shipping method you'd like to use?

Would you confirm the shipping address for me?

Would you mind giving me the account number again?

Sure. It's ZX 38927.

No problem. It's Smedley, account number 78631.

We'd like to use air freight, please.

Please deliver it to FFF Ltd.

Choose the correct words in these sentences.

1 Can I take some details *of* / *from* you?
2 Would you *confirm* / *to confirm* the shipping address for me?
3 *No* / *Not* problem. It's 99302.
4 Can I *check* / *checking* which shipping forwarder you want us to use?
5 Please deliver it *to* / *at* Jessop plc.
6 Could I *to have* / *have* your account number?
7 *We'd* / *We're* like to use air freight, please.
8 Would you mind *give* / *giving* me the account number again?
9 I'd like *check* / *to check* some details.
10 Could you *tell* / *tell me* what shipping method you'd like to use?

Language file 2 — Dealing with shipping problems

Complaining

There's a slight problem with the order we received today.

I'm expecting an order of 150 tables, but it hasn't arrived yet.

We ordered 130 jackets, but we've only received 100.

We've received 50 cases of small cups and no large ones.

Apologizing

Oh, dear, sorry about that.

Sorry to hear that.

I'm sorry you haven't received it.

I'm very sorry about that, I don't know how that's happened.

I do apologize.

Please accept our apologies.

Explaining

Your order was shipped on the thirteenth.

The order was shipped to the airport last night.

The item was out of stock so your order wasn't shipped.

According to the computer, it was loaded on a flight leaving this morning.

The computer's showing that it was shipped yesterday.

We sent it to your forwarder for sea freight.

We could only ship 100 last week, with the other 30 to follow.

We usually email to explain, but for some reason we didn't.

Promising action

I'll call the forwarder and find out for you.

I'll just check that we have the large ones in stock.

I'll arrange an urgent delivery by courier, so you should get them tomorrow.

They'll also collect the 20 cases that you don't want.

There'll be no shipping charge for that, of course.

Complete these sentences with the correct form of the verb in brackets.

1 I .... (receive) my order yesterday, but there .... (be) a slight problem with it.
2 I .... (call) the forwarders tomorrow, as their offices are closed today.
3 The order .... (ship) two days ago.
4 I .... (be) sorry you .... (not receive) it yet.
5 We .... (expect) an order but it .... (not arrive) yet.
6 I .... (not understand) what .... (happen).
7 We .... (send) it to your forwarder last week.
8 I .... (arrange) a courier collection if you'd prefer that.
9 The computer .... (show) that it .... (load) yesterday.
10 We .... (order) 60 jackets, but we .... (receive) 50.

Vocabulary file   Shipping methods

Complete the table with these shipping methods.

a air freight   b airmail   c courier   d motorcycle messenger   e sea freight

	Method	Advantages	Disadvantages
1		A fast service for letters and parcels, usually up to about 30 kg, to any destination in the world.	Cannot be used for very large or heavy items. No collection service.
2		A very fast service for sending smaller items in the same city or region. Items are collected from your office.	Expensive. Limited to smaller items and shorter distances.
3		Fastest service to all destinations. Very reliable. Collection service usually available.	Expensive. There can be problems overseas if the company uses smaller, local agents.
4		Economical and reliable service for very large overseas shipments.	Slow.
5		Fast and reliable service for large overseas shipments.	Expensive.

UNIT 12

Language file 1   Writing a summary

1 Read the text fairly quickly, to get a general understanding.

2 Read it again, in more detail, and highlight the important parts.

3 Write sentences based on the your highlighted sections.

4 Check that the sentences are clear – make them shorter where possible.

5 Check that everything is correct. If possible, ask a colleague to check, too.

Passive

Passive forms make a sentence feel less personal. They are used a lot in report writing, which should be less personal and more formal:

The ranking **was started** in 2000.
It **is predicted** that in the future we will see different media.

Present perfect

The present perfect is used to describe recent changes, and so is often used in report writing to describe recent trends:

Internet use **has risen** sharply in recent years.

Past simple

The past simple describes events at a point in past time:

Canada and Australia **were** also in strong positions.

Present continuous

The present continuous describes events around the present time:

Some **are progressing** more quickly than others.

Complete these sentences with the best form of the verb in brackets – past simple, present perfect or a passive form.

1 The World Wide Web .... (launch) in 1991.
2 Telecom companies' profits .... (fall) sharply in recent years.
3 Microsoft and Netscape .... (create) two different browsers in the 1990s.
4 Millions of web pages .... (add) to the Google search engine since it .... (introduce).
5 It .... (predict) that we will all have mobile Internet access in 20 years.
6 The number of 'Dot Com' companies .... (plummet) since 2001.
7 Local area networks allow multiple users .... (connect) to each other.
8 A lot of new anti-virus software .... (develop) in the 90s.

Vocabulary file   Trends and changes

	small changes	large changes
↗		
go up rise increase	slightly a bit a little	dramatically sharply a lot
shoot up rocket		dramatically sharply
↘		
go down fall decrease	slightly a bit a little	dramatically sharply a lot
dive nosedive plummet		dramatically sharply
→		
remain steady stay the same		

Look at the figures and choose the correct phrases to complete the sentences.

1 March: 4.25% → April: 4.3%
   Interest rates rose *sharply / slightly* in April.
2 1999: £1,500 → 2000: £650
   The average cost of a new computer *plummeted / rocketed* in 2000.
3 1995: 6 million → 2005: 4.8 million
   The population has *fallen / risen* sharply in the last ten years.
4 Last month: €6,000 → This month: €6,000
   Profits have *risen slightly / remained steady* this month.
5 Yesterday: 975p → Today: 368p
   The share price *nosedived / shot up* today.
6 May: $68 million → August: $99 million
   Sales increased *dramatically / slightly* as a result of the summer ad campaign.
7 2003: £115,000 → 2004: £116,000
   The average house price went up *a lot / a bit* in 2004.
8 1999: 48 hours → 2003: 38 hours
   Average working hours have *decreased / increased* a lot since the new legislation came in.

Language file 1   Asking questions after a presentation

Complimenting the speaker

I'd like to say I think your ideas are excellent.
Thank you for a very interesting talk.
I thought your suggestions were very original.

Leading up to a question

You mentioned that this model might not be practical for all types of brands.
You talked about four different approaches to the problem.
You said your company has experienced this before.

One thing you said was: 'Brand loyalty is often overestimated.'
One point you raised was that the markets are not stable at the moment.
One issue you touched on was a lack of financial backing for the project.

I'm not sure I quite understood your point about losing market position.
I don't know if I followed what you said about internal competition.

Asking for clarification

Could you give an example of a brand where it might not work so well?
Could you just explain again why that happened?
Could you clarify what you did as a result of that?
Can I just ask what you meant by that?

> Put the words in these sentences in the correct order.
>
> 1 successful / a / example / you / of / give / Could / campaign / an ?
> 2 possible / be / may / mentioned / this / always / that / You / not
> 3 to / presentation / was / think / excellent / like / I / I'd / your / say
> 4 what / that / meant / ask / Can / you / by / just / I ?
> 5 a / found / I / interesting / it / talk / very
> 6 weak / raised / that / economy / the / point / One / was / is / you
> 7 next / happened / you / Could / what / clarify ?
> 8 advertising / understood / not / I / quite / your / I'm / point / sure / about

Language file 2   Giving a presentation

Getting started

Thank you very much for coming.
My name's Alison Ellis.
I work for DFSL.
And just to remind you, my presentation today is called ...

Outline

My presentation today is in three main parts.
My talk will be in three main parts.

I'll start by discussing ...
Firstly, ...
Then I'll go on to ...
Secondly, ...
Thirdly, ...
Finally, I'll discuss ...
Lastly, ...

Main body

So, firstly, ...
OK, to begin, let's look at some figures.

And that brings me to the second and central part of my talk.
And that brings us to my next point.
So, let's move on to some examples.

As you can see on this transparency, ...
This graph shows ...

I could say a lot more about that, but now I'd like to explain ...
I could say a lot more about this, but time is moving on, so I'll turn to ...

Well, what is a brand?
So, why was it happening and what did we do about it?

Conclusion

So, to summarize, we started off by looking at ...
Let me sum up then.

Firstly, we looked at ...
Secondly, ...
Last but by no means least, ...
I believe that ...
And that brings me to the end of my presentation.

Are there any questions?
Does anyone have any questions?

Correct the mistakes in these sentences.

1 Thank you very much for come here today.
2 And just remind you, my talk is called ...
3 OK, for begin, let's think about past history.
4 I could say lot more about that, but now ...
5 So, to summary, we started off by looking at ...
6 Are there any question?

110

Language file 1   Talking about a company

What does your company do?
What line are you in?
What does that involve?

Leisure consultancy is our core business.
We aim to help companies.
I deal with a wide range of organizations.
We provide a service tailored to the client.
I'm often called in when ...
We offer a complete package.

We usually offer to analyze the services available.
My department's in charge of market research.
That's my speciality.
I work in other areas, too.
We try and come up with solutions.
We try to develop a plan based on the existing situation.
We find that most of these problems aren't big ones.
Our strategy is to ...

Match the halves to make complete sentences.

1	We try to develop	a	of the central region.
2	We provide technical	b	up with affordable suggestions.
3	What line	c	that customers will pay more for better service.
4	We try and come	d	is our core business.
5	We deal	e	is your company in?
6	Contract maintenance	f	support for office systems.
7	We're in charge	g	with a lot of small local businesses.
8	What does	h	to respond within 24 hours.
9	We aim	i	a client-based strategy.
10	We find	j	your role involve?

Language file 2   Organizational culture

purpose/goal/aim (n) + *to* + infinitive

Our (ultimate) purpose is to provide an affordable quality product.
Our (ultimate) goal is to satisfy our customers.
Our (ultimate) aim is customer satisfaction.

aim / seek / campaign / be determined + *to* + infinitive (*by* + *-ing*)

We aim to contribute to society by investing in local communities.
We aim to deliver a quality service.
We seek to offer a friendly, courteous and efficient service.
We will campaign to secure more protection for consumers.
We are determined to minimize our impact on the environment.

be committed to + *-ing*/noun

We are committed to offering comprehensive training.
Our organization is committed to high standards of service to customers.

believe that + subject + verb

The Co-op believes that it is wrong for many of the world's citizens ...

believe in + noun

This company believes in equality and fairness for all its employees.

Choose the correct words in these sentences.

1 We aim *improvement / to improve* our products constantly.
2 Our company *determines / is determined* to provide the best service.
3 I aim *to deliver / to delivering* a quality service.
4 We seek *offering / to offer* the lowest prices in town.
5 Our ultimate purpose is *increase / to increase* our profits.
6 We are committed *to selling / to sell* high quality food.
7 Our airline is committed to *total comfort / totally comfortable*.
8 My ultimate aim is *the satisfied customers / satisfied customers*.
9 I believe that *low prices / low prices are important*.
10 We believe in *low prices / low prices are important*.

Type of company:	limited company / public limited company	charity; trust	co-operative
Management:	director(s)	council of trustees; board of governors	co-operative members
Staff:	paid employees	paid employees and unpaid volunteers	employees are co-operative members or partners
Money that the company makes:	profit	surplus	profit + profit sharing
People who put money in:	investors	donors	
Money that people put in:	investment	donations	
Parts of a company that people own:	shares		
People who own parts of a company:	shareholders		

Complete these job advertisements with words from above.

Why would anyone work in one of our shops? All our shop workers are
(1) ...., so you won't get paid! But you will be supporting Europe's
biggest (2) ...., and helping poor people. We need more than just financial
(3) .... – we depend on our shops. So call us now and find out more!

Would you like to work for a company where the
(4) .... don't all go into the boss's pocket?
Where you will be a (5) ...., helping to
make decisions, and not just an employee? We offer good
working conditions and a generous (6) ....
scheme, so the more successful the company is, the more
you earn. Visit our website for more information.

You only have to look at our stock market listing to see how successful we
are: all smart (7) .... are (8) .... in our
company. As Britain's largest retail (9) ...., we can offer you
an excellent salary and benefits package, including a discount on any
(10) .... that you choose to buy in the company.
What are you waiting for? Email now!

Language file 1   Talking about company changes

Explaining changes

We want to keep you in the picture.
I've been asked to update you.
I want to keep everyone up-to-date.
I'd like to keep you informed.

I've been told that it's still under discussion.
We've been told that most people won't have to travel much further.

I can reassure you that nobody will lose their job.
There has been a new development regarding restructuring plans.
We are going to move to smaller sites, which will mean relocation for some of us.

Just to give you an idea, you may find that your job title changes slightly.
As far as I know, we're hoping for a five-year guarantee on job security.

Asking about changes

You say that Mackenzie is keeping the workforce ...

Does that mean our jobs are secure?
Does it mean we might have to travel to the other side of the city?

How will the relocation affect us?
What does it mean for our salaries?
What will happen if our job changes a lot?

a   Match the halves to make complete sentences.

1	There has been a new	a	will mean better job security.
2	We'd like to	b	an idea, we have had two bids.
3	Just to give you	c	told that it's still under discussion.
4	I've been asked	d	everyone informed.
5	As far as	e	development regarding the takeover.
6	I can reassure	f	you that it's all going to plan.
7	We want to keep you	g	to update you.
8	We're merging with DSL, which	h	keep you in the picture.
9	I'd like to keep	i	up-to-date.
10	I've been	j	we know, KHK aren't interested.

b   Match the halves to make complete questions.

1	Does it	a	it mean for the part-time workers?
2	How will	b	if the acquisition doesn't go through?
3	What does	c	mean some branches are going to close?
4	Does that mean	d	the merger affect office staff?
5	What will happen	e	we'll have to work longer hours?

Verbs	Nouns
Telco has announced that it is going to **acquire** the Best Buy retail chain.	This **acquisition** will make Telco the market leader.
It seems likely that Happy Foods will be **taken over** by the giant Meddlers plc.	This kind of **takeover** is the only way such a small company can survive today.
Meddlers is going to **bid** even more for Happy Foods.	Analysts believe Happy Foods will accept Meddlers' higher **bid**.
Space Broadcasting has **merged** with Planet Communications.	This latest **merger** makes Space/Planet the biggest in Europe.
Superjet and Flyme are **joining up** to operate a new European shuttle service.	This **joint venture** is necessary as both companies are too small to open such a major new route alone.
LDG is planning to **relocate** to a cheaper, out-of-town industrial unit.	**Relocation** may be the answer to LDG's problems.
Farms are being told to **diversify** if they want to survive.	The government has announced generous schemes to help with **diversification**.
BigTel is going to **restructure** its call centre operations.	BigTel says that the **restructuring** is vital in order to reduce costs.

Complete these news stories with words from above in the correct form.

1
The Royal Bank of Scotland (RBS) has .... American bank Charter One for $10.5 billion. RBS now plans to .... Charter One into Citizens to create one of the ten biggest banks in the US. RBS became the second largest bank in the UK in 2000, when it .... NatWest.

2
Troubled airline Alitalia wants to start a cost-cutting .... plan, but unions have refused to accept plans to cut jobs.

3
US cable TV firm Comcast, which launched a $66bn .... for Disney in February, has now scrapped its .... plans as Disney showed 'no interest' in the deal.

4
Air France and KLM have ...., in a deal which will form the world's biggest airline by sales. The airlines hope this .... will cut costs.

5
Irish firm Tullow Oil is going to .... South African rival Energy Africa in a $500m deal which will create one of the biggest oil firms focused on west Africa.

Language file 2   Cause and effect

Consequently, part-time workers don't make themselves ill.
As a result, everyone can afford to take some time off.

As a result of new legislation, everyone's working week was reduced.
Because of recent legislation, our company now offers paid holidays to all employees.
Because of this, employees are spending more time with their family.

A consequence of that is happier employees.
A negative effect for the company is that it costs more.

It means that men don't fall asleep at their desks.
It has caused bad feeling among some of the male employees.
This has resulted in cost-cutting in other areas.

Rewrite the second sentences using the words in brackets.

1 The two companies have merged. 100 people will lose their jobs. (consequently)
   Consequently, 100 people will lose their jobs.
2 New legislation has come in. Nobody works more than 35 hours. (result)
3 The new director wants to cut costs. There might not be any more overtime. (means)
4 The company opened its own gym two years ago. Some employees are much fitter now. (consequence)
5 The company is not making enough profit. They want us to be more efficient. (because)
6 All the senior management are men. There is friction with some female employees. (caused)
7 The newly merged company needs to reduce costs. It is restructuring its administration processes. (resulted)
8 We recently opened a new staff restaurant. Staff spend too long there! (negative)

Vocabulary file 2   Company benefits

annual holiday/leave	a number of weeks off work each year for holidays
sick leave	time off work when you are ill
unpaid leave	time off work for a particular reason; the company doesn't pay you, but your work is done by someone else while you are away, and your job is kept open for you
maternity leave	time off work before and after you have a baby
paternity leave	time off work for the father of a new baby
flexible hours	the company lets you organize when you work according to your family life
pension	money you receive when you retire, because you and/or your company pay in regular amounts when you are working

Choose words from above to match these situations.

1 My wife's going to have a baby next month.
2 I really don't feel well today; I don't think I can go to work.
3 From 5 o'clock this afternoon, that's it – two weeks of sun, sea and sand!
4 I need to start putting some money aside for when I retire.
5 I've enrolled on a college course. It's full-time for six months – it'll be like going back to school!
6 I had my baby two weeks ago.
7 My mother isn't well and I need to visit her three times a day.

Transcripts

UNIT 1 PART A

1

1

RECEPTIONIST:	Hello, Logica.
ROB:	Hello. I'd like to speak to the Human Resources Director, please.
RECEPTIONIST:	Who's calling, please?
ROB:	It's Rob Stephens.
RECEPTIONIST:	Thank you. Can I ask what it's about?
ROB:	My company supplies health insurance. I'm sure your company would be interested.
RECEPTIONIST:	I'm sorry, but the director is busy today. Could I take a message?
ROB:	No, it's OK, thanks. I'll call again.

2

RECEPTIONIST:	Good morning. GSK. Can I help you?
ROB:	Can I speak to the Human Resources Director, please?
RECEPTIONIST:	Can I ask who's calling, please?
ROB:	Yes, this is Rob Stephens from Direct Health Insurance.
RECEPTIONIST:	Thank you. I'll put you through.
ROB:	Thanks.

3

RECEPTIONIST:	Standard. Good morning.
ROB:	Hello. Could I speak to Neil Watson, please?
RECEPTIONIST:	Could I have your name, please?
ROB:	It's Rob Stephens from Direct Health Insurance.
RECEPTIONIST:	Is Mr Watson expecting your call?
ROB:	No. I'm calling to introduce our company's products.
RECEPTIONIST:	Well, I'm afraid Mr Watson isn't available at the moment. Could you send a brochure, and he can call you if he's interested?
ROB:	OK. I'll put one in the post.

UNIT 1 PART B

2

1

STUART:	Hello. Stuart Jones.
MIKE:	Hi, Stuart. It's Mike. How are you?
STUART:	Hi, Mike. Not bad, thanks. And you?
MIKE:	Fine, thanks. I was just calling to see if you got the catalogues I sent you.
STUART:	Oh, yeah. Thanks. They arrived yesterday. Have you got any more?
MIKE:	I'll check for you. Bye!

2

HUGH:	Hello. Hugh speaking.
KAREN:	Hi, Hugh. How are you?
HUGH:	Er ... fine thanks.
KAREN:	Good. I heard you were sick last week.
HUGH:	I'm fine now, thanks.
KAREN:	And is your wife better, too?
HUGH:	Yes ... Sorry, who's calling?
KAREN:	Oh, this is Karen.

3

LUKE:	Hello. Luke Young speaking.
STEVE:	Hi, Luke. Steve here.
LUKE:	Oh, hi, Steve. How are you?
STEVE:	Not bad, thanks. And yourself?
LUKE:	Can't complain. Busy though.
STEVE:	Yeah, it's that time of year.
LUKE:	Right.
STEVE:	The summer holidays seem a long time ago now, don't they?
LUKE:	Er, yeah they do.
STEVE:	When are you planning to have another holiday?
LUKE:	I don't really know. Um, what can I do for you, Steve?

4

ANNA:	Hello. Anna speaking.
SARAH:	Hi, Anna. It's Sarah. Can we meet next week to discuss your account?
ANNA:	Oh. Er, yes, sure, when did you want to meet?
SARAH:	How about Tuesday?

3

MARCO:	Hello. Marco Delta.
CHRIS:	Hi, Marco. Chris here.
MARCO:	Oh, hi, Chris. How are things?
CHRIS:	Not bad, thanks. And yourself?
MARCO:	Busy, but I can't complain. What can I do for you?
CHRIS:	Have you got a copy of the latest sales figures?
MARCO:	Yes. Shall I email them to you?

CHRIS: That would be great, thanks very much.
MARCO: No problem.
CHRIS: Right, I'll let you get on. Bye for now.
MARCO: Bye, Chris.

UNIT 2 PART A

1

INTERVIEWER: John, is it true to say that the use of email has made the business world less formal?

JOHN: Well, there's no doubt that written business communication has been revolutionized in recent years. Most business letters have been replaced by email because it's faster, cheaper and simpler, and this increased use of email for business communication has definitely made business writing less formal. But that doesn't mean that you should suddenly start being very informal with important customers. You still need to treat your customers politely, but email is so quick and convenient that we can easily forget to be polite. We should always use a greeting to open an email, and add a 'signature' at the end that offers other ways for people to contact us, such as a phone number. Remember, you should always be polite.

UNIT 3 PART A

2

1

MARK: ... With all the new offices that are opening around the region, I wonder if we could communicate a bit better.

SONIA: Yes, I'm worried that some of our people are feeling isolated. We want them to feel like part of the team.

EVA: Well, how much contact do you have now?

MARK: We mainly rely on email. But I think this is too impersonal. I think everyone wants to hear a voice occasionally. We telephone everyone about once a week, but this is expensive and not ideal.

EVA: Have you considered video-conferencing?

SONIA: Aha! I've thought about it, but it's very expensive.

EVA: What about video-conferencing on the Internet? That's much cheaper.

SONIA: I'm not familiar with it. Is it straightforward?

MARK: I've played with the software. It's quite easy to set up and use. I think we could install the software on computers in our offices quite quickly.

EVA: OK, let's look at that then. I think it could be a cheap way for us to have face-to-face meetings on a more regular basis.

2

EVA: Some of the offices are complaining that the product information sheets are arriving too late. Is there anything we can do to speed this up?

MARK: At the moment we're printing the sheets here and then mailing them to the offices. It takes time to print them out and then make copies.

SONIA: Could we email them to the offices as PDF files? The offices could then print them out and make copies themselves.

EVA: That sounds like a good solution. Could you ask the offices if they'd prefer to receive the sheets by email? They'd get them much more quickly. Of course, we need to check that they can make copies easily ...

UNIT 3 PART B

2

DIETER: If you ask me, our reps in Paris, Madrid, Portugal and Rome should be communicating much more with each other. At the moment, they all communicate directly with us here in Bonn. I think sharing ideas with each other would make them feel more like part of a team. What do you think?

SANDRA: I couldn't agree more. The question is how they communicate. Ideally, they should meet once a month.

DIETER: I suppose so, but that would be expensive. I think they should meet once every three months, and then we should encourage them to send emails to each other, sharing ideas or asking for suggestions, etc.

SANDRA: Yeah, as long as they don't spend all day reading and writing emails. Some kind of weekly exchange would be fine.

DIETER: Good point. Perhaps we could help them to set up video-conferencing on the Internet. This would allow them to have real-time, face-to-face meetings to follow up on the email exchanges, for example at the end of every month.

SANDRA: Yes, good idea. Let's look into that.

UNIT 4 PART B

2

INTERVIEWER: ... I'm sure you're aware of the kind of projects we are involved in. So, what have you got to offer us? Why do you think we should employ you?

SARA: Well, I'm creative and dynamic – I think my track record in my current job proves that, and it also shows that I have good experience. I'm self-motivated and good at organizing my time. I also think I'm flexible in the way I plan my work, and I'm keen to learn.

INTERVIEWER: What do you think your negative points are? What might your current employer want you to improve?

SARA: Perhaps I don't always delegate as much as I should, but I'm working on this and I think I've improved a lot.

INTERVIEWER: Mmhm. What is it about this post that attracts you?

SARA: I think this post offers a good opportunity to develop my skills, with a company which is obviously moving forward fast in fields that I'm interested in.

INTERVIEWER: And where do you see yourself five years from now?

SARA: Well, I'm ambitious but realistic. Right now I think I'm certainly capable of managing project teams. With the right experience, and further training of course, I would like to be the manager of a whole division in five years. I hope to climb the career ladder as fast as I can. But it's hard to say, isn't it?

INTERVIEWER: Yes, of course. Er, have you ever used the Quaddro system?

SARA: Yes, I have. I haven't used it in my current job, as the company uses Mekra. But I used Quaddro in my previous job, when I worked for LMH, from 2000 to 2002.

INTERVIEWER: All right. Do you have any questions for me?

SARA: Yes, I have one or two written down here ... I know you have a programme of staff training – what would that involve in the case of this position?

INTERVIEWER: Right. You would start with an induction programme, which consists of a series of half-day and one-day sessions, and ...

UNIT 5 PART A

2

1

EMPLOYEE: Excuse me, Mike. Could I leave a bit early tonight? It's my daughter's birthday.

MANAGER: No problem.

2

EMPLOYEE: I have to go to the dentist and she's only available this afternoon. Is it OK if I take a couple of hours off?

MANAGER: Well, I suppose so, if it's important. But you'll have to make up the time.

3

EMPLOYEE: I know you wanted the report by Monday, but do you mind if I give it to you on Wednesday?

MANAGER: Well, I really need it before Wednesday's meeting. Can I have it by Tuesday?

4

EMPLOYEE: I was wondering if I could work at home tomorrow. I've got to write the annual report and I can concentrate better at home.

MANAGER: Sorry, John, but I'm not in tomorrow, so I'd really like you to be here if that's OK.

EMPLOYEE: OK.

5

EMPLOYEE: Can I make a personal phone call? It's local.

MANAGER: Well, OK, but make it a quick call, please.

EMPLOYEE: Thanks.

3

1

KEN: Jane, I've got a bit of a problem.

JANE: Oh, dear. What is it?

KEN: I need to take my daughter to school in the mornings for a couple of weeks, and I was wondering if I could come in a bit later than usual.

JANE: That could be a problem. What time will you come in?

KEN: At 9.15. I can work later in the evening, if that's OK.

JANE: I'm sorry, Ken. The problem is that the regular meetings often start at 9.00. Is there any other way round it?

KEN: I'll see what I can do.

2

SARAH: Paul, do you have a minute?

PAUL: Sure. What is it?

SARAH: Could I leave a bit early today?

PAUL: I suppose so. Anything wrong?

SARAH: No, nothing's wrong. I have a dentist's appointment, that's all.

PAUL: OK. What time do you need to leave?

SARAH: About 4.45.

PAUL: Fine. No problem.

SARAH: Thanks a lot.

UNIT 5 PART B

2

1 When new clients come to visit us for the first time, I always meet them personally. I think this helps to create a good impression of the company, by showing them that they are important to us, and establishing a personal relationship with them from the beginning.

2 I always do the monthly departmental progress report myself. I'm the only person who has a good view of everything: what each individual team member is doing, and the effect of each individual's work on the progress of the whole team.

3 I never do progress reports on specific areas within the department. The individual team members are experts in their areas, and I don't know enough about all the details of their work, so I delegate that task to them and it seems to work pretty well.

4 I always ask someone else in the team to take minutes of meetings. That leaves me free to take a full part in the meeting, and afterwards I don't have to spend a lot of time writing the minutes – I just have to check what the team member has written before the minutes are circulated to everyone.

3

1

MANAGER: Howard, could you do something for me this morning?

HOWARD: I'm a bit busy right now, but I could do it in about an hour. What is it?

MANAGER: Would you contact all the Sales Managers and ask them if they'd be available for a meeting next week about the new sales campaign?

HOWARD: Sure. What day do you want to have the meeting?

MANAGER: Any day except Wednesday. Can you get back to me when you've set it up?

HOWARD: OK. I'll let you know when I've heard from everyone.

MANAGER: Thanks.

2

MANAGER: Jenny, I was wondering if you could do some research for me.

JENNY: Probably, yes. What exactly is the research?

MANAGER: Do you think you could find out about web design companies?

JENNY: Er, yes, I think I could ... but how soon do you need it?

MANAGER: Well, as soon as possible – when could you do it?

JENNY: I could start next week, and then it would take at least a couple of weeks.

MANAGER: That would be all right. Can you report back in a month?

JENNY: Sure. I'll do that.

UNIT 6 PART A

2

PAULA: Marco, is this a good time to give you some feedback on the Simba project?

MARCO: Sure.

PAULA: OK. Well, first of all, everyone would like to thank you very much for all your hard work.

MARCO: Not at all. It was a very enjoyable project to work on.

PAULA: Good! It's a big success – sales are already very good.

MARCO: Excellent. I'm glad to hear that.

PAULA: We were pleased that you set realistic targets – this enabled everyone to meet their deadlines and keep the project on schedule.

MARCO: I was, too. That can be quite hard sometimes.

PAULA: Yes, it certainly can. It was also good that you dealt with problems quickly, and came up with sensible solutions.

MARCO: Well, as you know, I like the problem-solving side of things.

PAULA: Yes. Now, of course, there are always areas which can be improved.

MARCO: Sure, of course.

PAULA: As you know, the project went over budget. Spending control could have been better.

MARCO: Yes, the budgets are so tight these days ... Have you got any suggestions for dealing with that?

PAULA: Well, for example, you could have more frequent budget reviews, to identify potential overspends before they get too big, and make adjustments.

MARCO: Yes, that's a good idea. Thanks for that.

PAULA: And another point to think about: some team members didn't always know what was happening. You need to improve team communication.

MARCO: Mmm, well, it was a big project team. What could I do about that?

PAULA: Have you thought of sending out weekly email updates to the whole team? That way you keep everyone informed without interrupting them unnecessarily.

MARCO: No, but that sounds good. I'll try that next time.

PAULA: OK. And that's it really. As I said, it was a very successful project and overall we're very pleased with what you did.

MARCO: Thank you. There's always room for improvement, isn't there?

PAULA: Well, it's good to try new ways of doing things. Do you have any questions or comments for me?

MARCO: Hmm ... well, I think you've covered everything ...

UNIT 6 PART B

 1

A: ... Now of course, even on the most successful projects there are things which could go better.

B: Yes, sure.

A: I think you already know that some of the newer team members felt they needed more support.

B: Yes, that's true. I'm sorry about that. In future, I'll plan extra training for people who aren't so familiar with the process.

A: Yes, I think that would be a good idea.

2

A: ... Good. Now, another thing is, I think you need to improve communication between team members.

B: Um, I'm not exactly sure what you mean. Can you give me specific examples?

A: Yes, sure. For example, at one point Nigel had to wait for parts to come from suppliers. He emailed Tim and phoned him, but he didn't get a reply for a week. If you establish a clear system of communicating between the parts buyers and the production side ...

3

A: ... and so you might want to think about that for next time.

B: Yes, that sounds good. Thanks very much.

A: And another point to think about is meeting deadlines. There were quite a few delays, and you missed some important deadlines.

B: I'm not sure that's entirely fair. I did my best but we didn't always receive the information that we needed on time. And we did say at the beginning that this might be a problem.

A: OK, perhaps we should go through the specific dates and analyze which deadlines were missed, and why.

B: Yes, please, I'd like to do that.

UNIT 7 PART A

 1

A: Did you hear about those two guys who started Google?

B: No, what about them?

A: They've both become billionaires now.

B: Really? Where did you hear that?

A: In the paper. They're in *Forbes* magazine's list of billionaires.

B: Imagine having all that money!

2

A: Hey, this is interesting ...

B: What's that?

A: easyJet's passenger numbers have gone up.

B: That doesn't surprise me, actually.

A: Why?

B: Well, I heard they were hoping to make a good profit this year.

UNIT 7 PART B

3

NICK: Sarah, I've got to travel up north for the conference next month – do you know how to get there?

SARAH: No, sorry, but have you tried the Traveline website?

NICK: No, I haven't.

SARAH: Well, you can find out about bus, coach and train times, and choose the best way.

NICK: Mmm ... is it complicated?

SARAH: No, it's really easy! There's a facility to search for your town or, if you prefer, there's a clickable map of the UK.

NICK: OK ... but what if I want more detailed information about a particular bus or train company?

SARAH: Easy again! There are links to the train and coach companies for their specific journey planners.

NICK: Right, I'll have a go. What's the web address?

SARAH: It's www.traveline.org.uk. That's it. So, first decide which way you want to start planning the journey, then you can choose what ...

UNIT 8 PART A

3

TONY: So, we can see from the figures that sales of the Max Fun are falling. It's our most popular model, so we really need to do something about it.

CLARE: Do we know why sales are falling, Tony?

TONY: Well, we have some ideas, but nothing very concrete yet. The first step would be to do some market research, I suppose. Ana, as Marketing Director, this is down to you, isn't it?

ANA: Yes, that's right. I'll get my team to organize some research – find out what people like and don't like about it, if there are other models they prefer and why, and so on. It'll take a bit of time, though.

TONY: How long will you need?

ANA: Well, at least a month, preferably six weeks.

TONY: OK. Let's make a note – Ana, market research, by October 15th?

ANA: Yes, that should be fine.

JOHN: That will be very helpful, but I think we should be working on this while we wait for the market research.

TONY: I see your point, John, but what exactly?

JOHN: Well, for example, we could think about possible changes and provide costings for them, to see if they're possible.

CLARE: Yes, that's a good idea, John. What about different colours? The Max Fun is grey ... not very exciting!

JOHN: Mmm, very true. And we don't have a waterproof version. Why not get costings for that, too?

TONY: Yeah, we should. Sounds like a job for the Production Manager, Clare – can you do that?

CLARE: Sure. I'll get costings for, say, three different colours, and a waterproof version. I think I can do that in a couple of weeks – how about September 15th?

TONY: That'll be fine.

ANA: Another thing ... as part of the research we'll be looking at packaging, of course. Could we get some ideas for different packaging designs?

JOHN: Good idea. I'll get my design team onto that ... we'll need three to four weeks, though. Um, 1st October?

TONY: Yeah, that's OK. John ... Design Manager ... 1st October. Good. Well, some good ideas there, let's hope we can start ...

UNIT 8 PART B

3

ANNE-MARIE: Well, if you ask me, we need to reduce the number of employees. That's the best way to cut costs.

BEN: I'm not sure I understand what you mean, Anne-Marie. It costs money to make people redundant, and then, when things pick up, you haven't got the skilled workers you need. It would be better to make fewer products.

ANNE-MARIE: Sorry, Ben, I'm not quite with you. How would that help? If you reduce production, then you have to reduce employees, don't you?

BEN: Not necessarily. If we focus only on the products that sell really well, we could increase production of those, and we wouldn't have to lose so many employees. What do you think, Chris?

CHRIS: I'm not sure. Can we just go over what you're both saying? Ben, you're saying that by focusing on the bestsellers, we can reduce costs.

BEN: Basically, yes.

CHRIS: And Anne-Marie, you think we would make more savings by simply reducing the workforce.

ANNE-MARIE: Yes, more or less.

CHRIS: OK. I'd like to suggest that we do some research on this. Anne-Marie, can you look at staffing levels and come up with some suggestions?

ANNE-MARIE: Sure, no problem.

CHRIS: And Ben, at the same time I'd like you to look at the product range and see what savings would be made by re-focusing our efforts on the bestselling lines.

BEN: Yes, that sounds like a good idea.

CHRIS: Now, we need to think about dates for all of this. Er, let's have a look at the calendar ...

UNIT 9 PART A

 a

HARRY: OK. Over the next three months, the goal is to maintain sales of our services to current customers. I'm going to use the database to make a list of all the companies in my area who bought our services last year. If I call them all next week, I can start visiting the following week. I plan to visit all the companies in the next two months. That way, I should have time after that to go back and revisit the companies which are undecided.

b

URSULA: Good, thanks, Harry. Can I make a few suggestions? There's no need for you to access the database yourself. Susana can make the list you want. It's her job and she'll be much faster than you. That means you can start calling your biggest customers, who you already know, right away. Also, if you start visiting sooner, you could find time between appointments to make more appointments. But remember, these are already our customers. It won't be difficult to make appointments. Keep sending the information you collect back to Susana. If we don't keep the database up-to-date, we might lose track of who you've visited and who you haven't visited. And one last thing: if you divide up your area and concentrate your visits in smaller areas, you should find you're using your time more effectively and you're more likely to meet your deadline.

UNIT 9 PART B

a

NANCY: Good afternoon. Nancy speaking.

DAVE: Oh, hello. It's Dave Barton here, from Microplus.

NANCY: Hello, Dave. You're visiting us next month, aren't you?

DAVE: Yes, that's right.

NANCY: Did you receive the schedule I sent?

DAVE: Yes, I did. Thanks very much. I have some questions about it, actually. I was wondering if we could make some small changes.

NANCY: Oh, yes, I expect so. What would you like to change ...?

b

DAVE: ... I was wondering if we could make some small changes.

NANCY: Oh, yes, I expect so. What would you like to change?

DAVE: Well, first, would it be possible to put lunch back an hour, so that I can check in at the hotel first?

NANCY: That shouldn't be a problem. Let's say 12 o'clock arrive at hotel – Carol can take you there, then pick you up at 12.45, for lunch at 1.00.

DAVE: That's great. Thanks. Now, in the afternoon, the tour seems quite long and the meetings quite short. Do you think we could cut down the tour and put off one of the meetings until Wednesday?

NANCY: Yes, we can certainly cut down the tour ... let's see ... um, lunch is now at 1.00, so the tour will start at 2.00. That could go on till 3.30, I think. Now, putting off a meeting ... that could be difficult. It won't be possible to move your meeting with the MD, as he won't be here on Wednesday. But we can probably put the other one off. Shall we say, 3.30 to 5.00, meeting with MD?

DAVE: Fine, yes. That also gives me time to go back to the hotel before the city tour and dinner.

NANCY: Good. So, Wednesday?

DAVE: Well, it seems there are a lot of short meetings in the morning and a lot of free time in the afternoon.

NANCY: Yes, and we also want to move the Production team meeting from Tuesday if possible.

DAVE: Oh, yes. I wonder if we could do that in the afternoon, and put back the Purchasing Manager until the afternoon, too.

NANCY: Yes, I think we can. How about: 9 o'clock Design Manager, 10.30 Sales managers, 12.00 lunch. Then 1.00 Production team ...

DAVE: 1 o'clock Production team.

NANCY: And 2.30 Purchasing Manager, finishing at 4 o'clock.

DAVE: That sounds good. And it still leaves time for a bit of sightseeing before I head off to the airport at 6 o'clock.

NANCY: Good! I'll make those changes and send you a revised schedule.

DAVE: Thanks very much indeed. See you next month!

NANCY: Yes, I look forward to meeting you. Bye.

DAVE: Bye.

UNIT 10 PART B

1 LISA: Multiform software is known for its flexibility. It comes with a standard package of incredible graphics tools and a huge range of effects. It's possible to import almost any kind of text or picture files, and that's why it's commonly used by professional designers. Multiform has a reputation for being a complete all-in-one design package – there's no need to buy any other support software. And this reputation was achieved without expensive advertising. Multiform got its reputation mainly by word of mouth, relying on designers to tell each other how good the software is.

UNIT 11 PART A

2 SALLY: Good morning, TTL. Can I help you?

GEOFF: Good morning, yes, we'd like to place an order, please.

SALLY: Certainly. Can I just take some details from you?

GEOFF: Sure.

SALLY: All right. First of all, do you already have an account with us?

GEOFF: Yes, we do.

SALLY: Could I have your company name and account number?

GEOFF: Yes, it's Green and White Limited, and the account number is 551203.

SALLY: Just a moment ... And you are ... Geoff Green?

GEOFF: That's right.

SALLY: OK, Mr Green, what would you like to order?

GEOFF: Just one item – three cases of medium-sized boxes, the ones with our company name on.

SALLY: Er, that will be ... item number GWB 8592, medium-sized boxes, three cases?

GEOFF: GWB 8592, that's it.

SALLY: Can you give me your purchase order number, for reference?

GEOFF: Yes, that'll be TTL 1006.

SALLY: Thanks, TTL 1006. Could you tell me what shipping method you'd like to use?

GEOFF: Air freight, please.

SALLY: And can I check which shipping forwarder you want us to use?

GEOFF: Er, the usual, Express Air Forwarding.

SALLY: ... Express Air Forwarding. Would you confirm the shipping address for me?

GEOFF: Yes, our own address, Unit 6, North East Industrial Estate, Central Avenue, Pickford.

SALLY: OK, that's fine. I'll just go over that – it's three cases of medium-sized boxes, item number GWB 8592, order number TTL 1006, shipping by air freight via Express Air Forwarding, to Green and White, Unit 6, North East Industrial Estate, Central Avenue, Pickford. Is that all correct?

GEOFF: Yes.

SALLY: Good. The order's entered in the system now, and it should be dispatched by the end of the day.

GEOFF: Thanks very much.

SALLY: Thank you, Mr Green. Bye.

GEOFF: Bye.

UNIT 11 PART B

2 1

SUPPLIER: Hello, Customer Service Department. How may I help you?

CUSTOMER: Hi, I'm expecting an order of 150 tables, but it hasn't arrived yet.

SUPPLIER: OK. Could I have your account number, please?

CUSTOMER: Yes, it's 09823783 and the purchase order number was PO170802.

SUPPLIER: Thank you. One moment, please. Yes, your order was shipped on the thirteenth. We sent it to your forwarder for sea freight. I'm sorry you haven't received it, but you'll need to contact them. Do you have their number?

CUSTOMER: Yes, I do. I'll call the forwarder and find out where the order is.

SUPPLIER: OK. Thank you. Bye.

CUSTOMER: Bye.

2

SUPPLIER: Hello, Brookline.

CUSTOMER: Hello. I'm calling from KTS. We ordered 130 jackets, but we've only received 100.

SUPPLIER: Oh, dear, sorry about that. Let me just check ... Ah, I see, order number 88375. Due to low stock levels, we could only ship 100 last week, with the other 30 to follow shortly. We usually email to explain, but for some reason we didn't. I do apologize.

CUSTOMER: That's OK. When can I expect them?

SUPPLIER: Well, the order was shipped to the airport last night and according to the computer, it was loaded on a flight leaving this morning.

CUSTOMER: Thanks very much.

SUPPLIER: You're welcome. Bye.

CUSTOMER: Bye.

3

SUPPLIER: Hello, Shipping Department.

CUSTOMER: Hello. I'm calling from GDK Limited.

SUPPLIER: Oh, good morning.

CUSTOMER: Morning. There's a slight problem with the order we received today.

SUPPLIER: Sorry to hear that. What was the purchase order number?

CUSTOMER: 6736.

SUPPLIER: Just a moment ... Ah, yes, 10 cases of large cups, and 30 cases of small ones. Shipped on Wednesday. Is that right?

CUSTOMER: Yes, that's right, but three cases of large cups are damaged.

SUPPLIER: Oh, I'm very sorry about that, I don't know how that's happened. I'll organize replacements for you. I'll arrange an urgent delivery by courier, so you should get them tomorrow. There'll be no shipping charge for that, of course.

CUSTOMER: Great. Thank you.

SUPPLIER: The courier will also collect the damaged ones. Please accept our apologies.

CUSTOMER: Oh, that's all right. Thank you for sorting it out so quickly. Bye.

SUPPLIER: Bye.

UNIT 12 PART A

1 INTERVIEWER: Jenny, you train business people to write summaries and reports – a very important skill in today's business world, but not always easy. Just thinking about summaries first of all, what's the first step in writing a summary?

JENNY: Well, the first step isn't writing at all – it's reading! You should start by reading the whole text fairly quickly, to get a general understanding. Don't spend too long looking at the detail, just the general idea and the main points.

INTERVIEWER: And what's the second stage?

JENNY: Before you read it again, think carefully about what information your manager or your company wants and what is the most important thing for them. Then read the information again, in more detail, and highlight the important points.

INTERVIEWER: OK, that seems easy for written information, but what about charts and graphs? Should you just copy them into your summary?

JENNY: If they're clear and well presented, and all the information in them is useful for your summary, then yes – highlight the whole thing. But if you only want some of the information, just mark those parts that you want. Sometimes it's quicker and easier to summarize part of a graph in a simple sentence.

INTERVIEWER: How do you decide what information to put in and what to leave out?

JENNY: Well, the most important thing is to include general ideas and not too many details in a summary. Once you have the general idea and the main points, it helps to write a sentence for each point, keeping it as short and simple as possible. You can use headings, bullet points and lists rather than full sentences.

INTERVIEWER: What should you check when reading through your summary?

JENNY: Check that it's correct, clear and easy to understand. Cut out any sentences that don't give essential information. At the end of the summary, tell readers where they can find the full original report in case they want more details. Ask a colleague to read through your summary and make suggestions.

INTERVIEWER: OK, good. Well, that's very useful information indeed about summary writing. Now I'd like to move on to reports if we may ...

UNIT 13 PART A

② TIM: Thank you very much for coming, everyone. My name's Tim Harman, and I'm the Brand Manager for Mallory Products. And just to remind you, my presentation today is called 'Keeping it Going: Maintaining a Successful Brand'. My talk will be in three main parts. I'll start by discussing what exactly we mean by 'branding', and look at examples of some successful Mallory brands. Then I'll go on to a case study, and examine more closely what happened to one of our best brands, and what we did about it. Finally, I'll discuss how this practical example could perhaps form a model for successful maintenance of any brand, which I hope you may find useful in your own industries. So, firstly, what is a brand? Well, as with any business term, there are different definitions, which ...

③ TIM: ... and that brings me to the end of this presentation. Does anyone have any questions? Yes, the lady here at the front.

Q1: Yes. First, I'd like to say I think your ideas are excellent.

TIM: Thank you.

Q1: You mentioned that this model might not be practical for all types of brands ... could you give an example of a brand where it might not work so well?

TIM: Well, it seems to work well for our types of products, but perhaps if you were involved in marketing a less 'consumable' product type, for example, ...

Q2: I'm not sure I quite understood your point about losing market position. Could you just explain again why that happened?

TIM: Yes, sure. Glimmer, the market leader at the time, is a high quality product. But it wasn't cheap.

Q3: One thing you said was: 'Brand loyalty is often overestimated.' Can I just ask what you meant by that?

TIM: Yes. I think we often focus so much on establishing a brand that perhaps we assume our job is then finished. But consumers won't necessarily stay loyal to the brand ...

UNIT 13 PART B

② Extract 1

TIM: ... and that gives you an overview of our key products. So, as you can see, we have a number of leading brands to maintain. And that brings me to the second and central part of my talk. Our most successful brand, Glimmer, was the market leader in its segment for some years. This graph shows the kinds of sales figures it had, compared to the competition. But, in 2004, sales fell slightly. So, why was it happening and what did we do about it? Well, first of all, we had to ...

Extract 2

TIM: ... we had to make some difficult decisions about Glimmer, but of course we're pleased with the position it's in now. I could say a lot more about that, but now I'd like to explain how Glimmer can be used as a model for other business situations ...

Extract 3

TIM: ... but we can't really say for sure, and I'd be interested to hear feedback from any of you who choose to try out this approach. So, to summarize, we started off by looking at what a brand is ...

③ TIM: Thank you very much for coming, everyone. My name's Tim Harman, and I'm the Brand Manager for Mallory Products. And just to remind you, my presentation today is called 'Keeping it Going: Maintaining a Successful Brand'. My talk will be in three main parts. I'll start by discussing what exactly we mean by 'branding', and look at examples of some successful Mallory brands. Then I'll go on to a case study, and examine more closely what happened to one of our best brands, and what we did about it. Finally, I'll discuss how this practical example could perhaps form a model for successful maintenance of any brand, which I hope you may find useful in your own industries. So, firstly, what is a brand? Well, as with any business term, there are different definitions, which ...

... So, as you can see, we have a number of leading brands to maintain. And that brings me to the second and central part of my talk. Our most successful brand, Glimmer, was the market leader in its segment for some years. This graph shows the kinds of sales figures it had, compared to the competition. But, in 2004, sales fell slightly. So, why was it happening and what did we do about it? Well, first of all, we had to ...

... but of course we're pleased with the position it's in now. I could say a lot more about that, but now I'd like to explain how Glimmer can be used as a model for other business situations ...

... but we can't really say for sure, and I'd be interested to hear feedback from any of you who choose to try out this approach. So, to summarize, we started off by looking at what a brand is ...

... and that brings me to the end of this presentation. Does anyone have any questions? Yes, the lady here at the front ...

UNIT 14 PART A

3

AMY:	Excuse me, is anyone sitting here?
GEOFF:	No, please, go ahead.
AMY:	Thanks.
GEOFF:	I'm Geoff Anderson. Lincoln Solutions.
AMY:	I'm Amy Green from ALC. Pleased to meet you.
GEOFF:	Pleased to meet you, too. What does ALC do?
AMY:	We do various things, but, er, leisure consultancy is our core business.
GEOFF:	Ah, I see ... and what does that involve?
AMY:	Well, basically, we aim to help organizations provide the best leisure services possible. We offer a complete diagnosis and solution package.
GEOFF:	Business to business, then.
AMY:	Yes, very much. We deal with a wide range of organizations – local authorities, private leisure companies, fitness clubs. We provide a service tailored to the client.
GEOFF:	And, er, presumably they come to you because they want to increase business.
AMY:	Yes, the usual thing. We're often called in when a leisure provider isn't getting sufficient numbers through the door, and therefore not enough income. We usually offer to analyze the services available

and do some local market research at the same time, and see how well the two match up. My department's in charge of the market research side of things, so that's my speciality, but, er, I work in other areas, too.

GEOFF:	And then you try and come up with solutions?
AMY:	Yes, that's right. We try to develop a plan to increase customer numbers for our client. We find that most of these problems aren't big ones, they just need someone from the outside to look at the business and come up with small but significant improvements. What about Lincoln Solutions? What line are you in?
GEOFF:	Oh, well, we're in a very different field, but in many ways our strategy is very similar to yours ...

UNIT 14 PART B

1

ROB CARTER:	At Apex Advertising, the organizational culture is very important. For us, organizational culture is the way people in the organization understand, behave and act. It holds the organization and its employees together, and it influences the organization at every level. At Apex Advertising, we have worked for years to develop a culture focused on originality and creativity. The structure is very non-hierarchical. Everyone feels like part of a team, and is encouraged to contribute ideas and opinions. Our workplace is completely open-plan, with nobody working behind closed doors, from trainees to senior management.

UNIT 15 PART A

2 a

LOUISE:	Thanks for coming along, everyone. Now, as you know, our merger with Mackenzie is almost complete, and of course we want to keep you in the picture. We now have a bit more information, and I've been asked to update you with three pieces of news. Firstly, I can reassure you that nobody will lose their job – Mackenzie plan to continue with the existing workforce.

Secondly, there has been a new development regarding restructuring plans. Some of our operations are going to move to smaller sites, which will mean relocation for some of us, but not to other parts of the country. All operations will stay here in Bristol. And lastly, as part of the restructuring, there will be some changes in names of departments, and what each department is responsible for. But this won't substantially change the job that each of you does – um, just to give you an idea, you may find that your job title changes slightly. Right, that's everything, I think. I hope you agree that's all good news. Does anyone have any questions?

b

LOUISE: ... I hope you agree that's all good news. Does anyone have any questions?

Q1: Louise, thanks, that seems to be good news. Um, you say that Mackenzie is keeping the workforce – does that mean our jobs are completely secure forever?

LOUISE: Well, as far as I know, we're hoping for a five-year guarantee on job security. I've been told that it's still under discussion, but that Mackenzie will probably agree to it.

Q2: How will the relocation affect us? Does it mean we might have to travel to the other side of the city?

LOUISE: I'm afraid I don't know yet. We've been told that most people won't have to travel much further than they do at the moment, but we don't have any more details at this stage.

Q3: What will happen if our job changes a lot because of all the department changes? Will the company provide training?

LOUISE: Well, as I said, your job shouldn't change very much at all. But if there are any bigger changes to your work, Mackenzie will offer any necessary retraining. They're experienced in these mergers, and they've done that in the past.

Q4: What does it mean for our salaries? Will we have to take a pay cut?

LOUISE: No, absolutely not. Your conditions of employment won't change at all, and again we have reassurances from Mackenzie that existing pay agreements will be honoured.

UNIT 15 PART B

3

1 Last year, as a result of new legislation, everyone's working week was reduced to a maximum of 35 hours. This was the biggest change at our company for many years. I think it's great that no one stays late now, worrying about finishing a task. I'm sure that because of this, employees are spending more time with their family, or doing more sport, and a consequence of that is happier employees, who seem more relaxed and able to face the challenges of a working day. Obviously, a negative effect for the company is that it costs more financially, but there's no doubt that employees are more productive, so on balance I'd say it's been a positive change for everyone.

2 My company recently extended the amount of paid paternity leave it offers to 12 weeks. I think paternity leave is a good idea in principle, as we all know how important it is for the father to spend time with a new baby. And it means that men don't fall asleep at their desks, which used to happen! But it has caused bad feeling among some of the male employees, who make comments like, 'I've got no plans to become a father, so I can't have 12 weeks off. Why not?' So, overall, I don't think it's been a good thing for our company. It would be better to have some kind of 'family leave', which anyone could take for any reason, including the arrival of a new baby. That would seem fairer to me.

3 Because of recent legislation, our company now offers paid holidays to all employees, even those who are part-time. As a result, everyone can afford to take some time off for a break, and consequently, part-time workers don't make themselves ill working for long periods with no time off! It has been quite expensive for the company, though – not just paying for the holiday leave, but paying someone else to cover for a worker who is away, and then of course all the administration costs. This has resulted in cost-cutting in other areas, and price increases to our customers, which I don't think are a good thing. But overall, I think it's an improvement, as employees are being treated more fairly.

Acknowledgements

Mark O'Neil would like to thank the long-suffering members of his family in Japan who gave up their time to enable him to work on this project – his children, Talia, Clare, Kieran and Morris and his wife, Soko.

Gareth Knight is grateful to his colleagues at the Department of Linguistics, Srinakharinwirot University and ThaiTESOL for their support and understanding, and to his wife, Sasithorn, for her patience.

Bernie Hayden is indebted to his wife and children for their support and understanding during the many hours spent away from them working on the project.

The authors would like to express most sincere thanks to all the team at Cambridge University Press, in particular, Elin Jones, Clare Abbott, Sally Searby, Will Capel and Tony Garside for their unfailing calmness, patience and good humour, and their expert guidance at every stage.

Our thanks also go to Janaka Williams, Debbie Goldblatt, James Hunter and Bridget Green for their expert suggestions and also to Barnaby Pelter for his invaluable input.

The publisher would like to thank the following for permission to reproduce photographs.
Alvey & Towers for p. 49(br); Bildagentur Franz Waldhaesl / Alamy for p. 42(r); Anthony Blake Picture Library for p. 49(extreme br) Bob Cramp; Art Directors & TRIP for p. 48; Brand X Pictures / Alamy for pp. 42(l), 52(t); Courtesy of Canon for p. 49(extreme bl); Corbis for pp. 6(b), 10, 15, 38, 52(items a, b, c, e), 56, 66(tr); Getty Images for pp. 16, 24; Robert Harding Picture Library for p. 6(t); Colin Hawkins / Alamy for p. 52(item d); Imagestate / Alamy for p. 20; DK Khattiya / Alamy for p. 50(t); Powerstock for pp. 14(tl), 49(bl); Punchstock / Bananastock for p. 71, /Brand X Pictures for p. 66(tl), / Digital Vision for pp. 26, 54, /Image Source for p. 62, / Photodisc for p. 9; Courtesy of Siemens for p. 14(tr); Courtesy of Sony for pp. 14(b), 51; Tips Images for p. 45; Bob Turner / Alamy for p. 70; Zefa for pp. 28, 43.

For the screenshot on pp. 36 and 98 www.bloomberg.com with kind permission of Bloomberg L.P.; for the screenshot on p. 36 www.traveline.org.uk with kind permission of Traveline; for the screenshot on p. 36 www.infotel.co.uk with kind permission of Infotel Solutions; for the advertisement on p. 49 with permission of Lufthansa German Airlines; the BT logo on p. 49 with permission of British Telecommunications plc; for the Government statistics on pp. 59 and 81 from the National Statistics Website: www.statistics.gov.uk. Crown copyright material is reproduced with the permission of the Controller of HMSO; for the text and CO-OPERATIVE GROUP logo on pp. 68 and 69 with permission of the Co-operative Group; the Oxfam logo on p. 66 and the information about the organisation is reproduced here with the permission of Oxfam GB, 274 Banbury Road, Oxford, OX2 7DZ www.oxfam.org.uk. Oxfam GB does not necessarily endorse the activities that accompany the text; the GONGMAN logo on p. 66 with permission of Rank Leisure Holdings plc; the VOLVO logo on p. 50 with permission of Volvo Trademark Holding AB; the FUJI logo on p. 50 with permission of Fuji Photo Film (U.K.) Ltd; the MASTERCARD brandmark on p. 50 with permission of MasterCard International; the HILTON logo on p. 50 with permission of Hilton International Co.; the YAHOO! logo on p. 50 with permission of Yahoo! Inc; permission to use the Harley Davidson logo on p. 50 was given with the approval of Harley-Davidson Motor Company, The Bar & Shield logo is a registered trademark of H-D Michigan, Inc.; the Edinburgh Bicycle Co-operative logo on p. 66 with permission of the Edinburgh Bicycle Co-operative; the PUMA logo on p. 50 with permission of Puma UK.

The authors and publishers are grateful to the following for permission to use copyright material in Business Goals 3. While every effort has been made, it has not been possible to identify the sources of all the material used and in such cases the publishers would welcome information from the copyright owners.

Commissioned photography p. 6(b).

Picture Research by Kevin Brown

Illustrations by Kamae Design

146326